Feeling Like Crap

Young People and the Meaning of Self-Esteem

Nick Luxmoore

Jessica Kingsley Publishers
London and Philadelphia

First published in 2008
by Jessica Kingsley Publishers
116 Pentonville Road
London N1 9JB, UK
and
400 Market Street, Suite 400
Philadelphia, PA 19106, USA

www.jkp.com

Library of Congress Cataloging in Publication Data
Luxmoore, Nick, 1956-
  Feeling like crap : young people and the meaning of self-esteem / Nick Luxmoore.
    p. cm.
  Includes bibliographical references.
  ISBN 978-1-84310-682-1 (pb : alk. paper) 1. Self-esteem in adolescence. I. Title.
  BF724.3.S36L89 2008
  155.5'182--dc22

                              2007049950

British Library Cataloguing in Publication Data
A CIP catalogue record for this book is available from the British Library

ISBN 978 1 84310 682 1

Printed and bound in Great Britain by
Athenaeum Press, Gateshead, Tyne and Wear

Feeling Like Crap

by the same author

Working with Anger and Young People
Nick Luxmoore
ISBN 978 1 84310 466 7

Listening to Young People in School, Youth Work and Counselling
Nick Luxmoore
ISBN 978 1 85302 909 7

of related interest

Help Your Child or Teen Get Back On Track
What Parents and Professionals Can Do for Childhood Emotional and Behavioral Problems
Kenneth H. Talan, M.D.
ISBN 978 1 84310 870 2

Cool Connections with CBT
Encouraging Self-esteem, Resilience and Well-being in Children and Young People
Laurie Seiler
ISBN 978 1 84310 618 0

Nurture Groups in School and at Home
Connecting with Children with Social, Emotional and Behavioural Difficulties
Paul Cooper and Yonca Tiknaz
ISBN 978 1 84310 528 2
Innovative Learning for All series

For Morton
and
in memory of Olive

Acknowledgements

Earlier versions of these chapters have previously been published by King Alfred's College, Wantage, the Oxfordshire Learning Partnership and Refugee Resource, Oxford. I'm grateful to friends and colleagues who have read and commented on these versions.

I'd also like to thank colleagues who have shared ideas and expertise with me in supervision meetings and on training courses.

My enduring gratitude is to Kathy, Frances and Julia.

Contents

CHAPTER 1

Introduction

We use the word all the time. We say that one young person 'lacks self-esteem', that another 'suffers from low self-esteem' and another 'has self-esteem issues'. We say it. We write it. We seem to know what we mean. It sounds simple, as if these young people deemed to be 'lacking self-esteem' just need a bit of extra praise or to be taken aside and convinced that, really, they're not that bad. If they can somehow edge their way across the wobbly rope bridge, urged on by an instructor and a few muddy peers shouting encouragement from the riverbank below, then their 'self-esteem' will increase and they'll grow into confident citizens.

Of course, important work goes on all the time in schools, youth centres, hospitals, prisons – wherever dedicated, compassionate adults are supporting troubled and troublesome young people. And as part of that work, praise, reassurance, challenge and achievement all matter enormously. But it's rarely that simple. Ideas as complex as a young person's sense of self and sense of their own significance in the world are in danger of being reduced to a single word ('self-esteem') and, probably, to a brief set of interventions. When a young person's underlying 'self' is badly damaged or is incomplete in some way, our well-meaning attempts to bolster that person's 'self-esteem' can often make little impression.

This book explores how a young person's self might be constructed in the first place and what might help that self to feel more valued and confident in the world. What exactly *is* self-esteem and how do young people develop it?

There are conflicting accounts of the point at which a 'self' comes into existence. Some theorists describe an unconscious, archetypal 'self' buried inside each person, while others describe a predetermined self, a self we were born to become. Human biologists might describe an inherited, micro-biological 'self', complete with its own DNA, while Marxists might describe a 'self' created almost entirely by socio-economic circumstances. I like Kohut's (1977) observation that 'Demands for an exact definition of the nature of the self disregard the fact that "the self" is not the concept of an abstract science, but a generalisation derived from empirical data' (p.310). In other words, a 'self' isn't a thing in itself but is a way of understanding and describing our experience.

This book explores the idea of a socially constructed self, a self that's the product of relationships with other people, because that's the one which, in my experience, gets damaged by those relationships from the very beginning and that's the one which might, therefore, be repaired by other relationships later in life.

These reparative relationships don't have to involve busy professionals in years of work with only a few people. Young people are affected more by the quality than by the quantity of the time they get to spend with a professional and by that person's capacity to understand and help them think about themselves.

Being able to think about themselves matters hugely. When they're in trouble, we ask young people to go away and 'reflect' on their behaviour and we get frustrated when they can't. As I'll describe in Chapter 2, learning to reflect begins at birth when a baby sees itself reflected in the face of an attentive caregiver,[1] imitating and mirroring the baby back to itself. A sense of self emerges from these early interactions. Over time and having absorbed enough of this attention, the baby develops an ability to reflect *on itself* without needing another person. Verhofstadt-Deneve (2007) describes our eventual capacity to think thoughts and feel feelings while simultaneously observing and thinking *about* ourselves. Fonagy *et al.* (2004) describe this process as learning to 'mentalise' – the vital ability to think about and therefore regulate ourselves. When a baby hasn't learned how to do this, it falls to others, years later, to listen carefully and try to understand a grumpy fifteen-year-old baby, patiently helping it to reflect on itself.

Like many professionals, I work with young people whose formative relationships have affected their sense of who they are and who they can become; young people whose potential 'self-esteem' has already been adversely affected by relationships at home and at school. On a bad day, this can seem like hopeless work because by the time a young person is fourteen or fifteen years old (or even four or five years old) it's easy to conclude that the damage has been done: too much has already happened for any well-meaning adult to make much of a difference.

I don't agree. Whilst it's true that a lot of damage *has* often been done and an emergent 'self' may well have been battered and bruised in all sorts of ways, I think that professionals and other adults can amend the damage if they pay attention to the core processes which created that self in the first place. The lack of confidence, the self-loathing, defensiveness and hostility towards other people can be tempered. New possibilities can emerge from new relationships.

I work as the counsellor in a large comprehensive school, listening to all sorts of young people and helping them to reflect on themselves. However, the counselling service is integrated into the life of the school and I have a repertoire of involvements beyond individual counselling with students and staff. These involvements are intended to support the institution as a whole because, as I'll describe in Chapter 4, the experience of being in a school environment is at least as important for the development of a 'self' as individual counselling. I like working in schools because I think it's possible to create a culture which supports this development *in addition* to whatever individual attention young people may be getting. I've worked in youth centres and community settings where it's also possible to create that kind of prevailing culture.

This prevailing culture is effectively another kind of mirror in which a young person is recognised or ignored, welcomed or scorned. The experience of young asylum seekers testifies to the effect on a developing sense of self when the prevailing culture in a country of birth is hostile, even murderous. The work described in Chapter 3 took place, not in a school, but when I was working as a counsellor for a charity. Asylum-seeking young people with little or no English and with only a hazy understanding of what to expect from 'counselling' had to walk nervously up two flights of stairs, ring the doorbell, come in, speak to someone at the door and then walk across a large, sprawling office area where various workers they didn't know were sitting at desks... All this to get to the counselling room. So we spent a long time discussing how we should greet young people on this discouraging journey. Would it be respectful for the workers at their desks to take no notice? Would that be less intrusive for a very shy or disorientated young person? Would it make the journey to the counselling room more bearable? Or should the workers say hello?

My view was that the workers should always *look* to say hello, taking their cue from the young person, making eye contact when it was offered and saying a warm, respectful hello unless that was clearly unwanted. Pretending to take no notice might actually increase whatever sense of invisibility a young person might already be feeling. Saying hello would be normal. Saying hello would *recognise* the young person.

We exist in relation to other people and a sense of self develops only insofar as other people recognise and respond to us. Some therapists give nothing away about themselves, saying little, rarely interrupting silences and maintaining a neutral, opaque demeanour at all times. This approach may be useful for robust adults but for most young people it's too weird: the model has to be adapted because the danger is that a young person with an already shaky sense of self is left feeling even more shaky. Getting only a few cool, pithy interpretations from a parent-figure potentially increases the sense of fragmenting, of not really existing.

The charity I worked for undertook a rigorous two-year evaluation of its therapeutic service, eventually winning a national counselling award.[2] Asylum seekers and refugees who had used the service were asked all sorts of things including, obviously, what they had most appreciated about the service. Their replies were interesting. They didn't comment on our grasp of clinical technique, our theoretical understanding of trauma or our ability to work with the unconscious. Instead they said, 'I like it because the people are kind and friendly. They make me feel good.' The goings-on in the privacy of the counselling room were important, for sure, but the sense of simply being *recognised* by other human beings was just as important. It obviously mattered enormously that the prevailing culture was friendly and welcoming and that the other workers in the office said hello.

Working in a school, I come across young people in different contexts. The same student I saw for counselling behind closed doors in the morning I may later greet in the car park at lunchtime and sit with in a meeting after school about tackling homophobia. I learn everybody's names and say hello to as many people in the school as possible. This is important because part of my usefulness is to be what Lomas (1987) calls an 'environment therapist', constantly recognising young people, trying to understand what they tell me, keeping them company, being pleased to see them, helping to provide a safe enough environment in which they can move around, explore and grow. This exploration happens through individual counselling but it also happens outside the counselling room. It's provided by professionals working with young people in all sorts of other ways as well. Saying hello may not sound like much but it's the foundation from which a sense of self develops. A mother recognises her child. She gives it a name. She calls it by its name and is pleased to see it. She interacts with it and, when it cries, she listens, trying to understand.

This is essentially what professionals do. From good experiences in supportive cultures young people take not clever interpretations or startling insights but an abiding sense of being interesting and understandable despite all that's happened and may still be happening in their lives. And being understandable is profoundly reassuring. Holmes (2001) writes that 'Therapy begins – and ends – with finding a therapist "who understands how I feel"' (p.132). That therapist-who-understands could be a youth worker, a psychiatric nurse, a policewoman or, indeed, a parent. Therapeutic experiences don't happen only in 'therapy'.

So although this book is illustrated from my experience as a professional counsellor working with young people in schools, it's about trying to understand, *really* understand. What makes a difference to a young person with a shaky sense of self and described as having 'low self-esteem' is experiencing from professionals the kind of reflective mothering which recognises and understands what the fifteen-year-old baby is trying to say, thereby offering that baby new possibilities and amended ways of seeing the world. This book describes different ways in which a young person's self develops and gets damaged but then, with different kinds of recognition and understanding, pulls through. It describes ways in which these new possibilities develop.

This is far from easy. To begin with, I'm going to describe individual work with six young people, all different but all said to be 'lacking self-esteem'. Each account illustrates particular ways in which a 'self' emerges and gradually develops what might be called 'self-esteem'. And, because that 'self' is socially constructed, I'll go on to describe further work with these six young people, meeting together for four sessions as a group.

The first young person is Pete.

NOTES

1. Throughout this book, I shall refer to this caregiving presence as a 'mother' or as 'mothering', knowing full well that fathers also fulfil this function.

2. Refugee Resource (www.refugeeresource.org) received the 2006 national Award for Excellence in Counselling and Psychotherapy Practice, awarded by the British Association for Counselling and Psychotherapy.

CHAPTER 2

A Developing Self

PETE'S CRAP

Pete sits in my counselling room and, without looking up, starts eating his packed lunch two hours ahead of time. I ask how he's feeling.

'Like crap!'

'How come?'

'This school's crap! I can't wait to leave!'

'This school' is always a first line of defence for Pete. He goes on to tell me about useless teachers and pointless lessons but I'm interested in the 'crap'. The school is crap and Pete feels like crap. It may well be that he's just being lazy with his adjectives and can't be bothered to think of anything more precise. But I suspect that his experience of school is probably bound up with his sense of himself (see Chapter 4). It may be that, because he feels like crap, it makes school and everything else seem crap or that, because school really *is* crap, he feels *like* crap. Either he projects his own feelings onto school or his experience of useless and pointless school leaves Pete feeling useless and pointless himself.

The relationship between Pete and school is more personal than he would admit. As Chapter 4 describes, there's usually a connection between young people's feelings about 'school' and their feelings about 'mother' because, like a mother, school so powerfully provokes an expectation of nurture at the same time as it almost inevitably delivers an experience of some disappointment. For Pete, finishing his sandwich and hungrily starting a bag of crisps, 'school' is a constellation of all the things that he worries about, misunderstands and gets wrong. I suspect that this 'crap' school is an unconscious reminder of mothering which probably left Baby Pete feeling worried, misunderstood and somehow 'wrong' fifteen years ago. 'I can't wait to leave school!' might be his way of saying, 'I can't wait to get rid of the part of myself which feels useless!' because, when young people leave school, something *does* change: the physical environment, the daily routines are different and 'It feels weird not being at school!' Hundreds of young people leaving school are in limbo until something else becomes the crapness in their lives and they can look back on school more benevolently because it no longer represents a part of themselves that they despise.

But, in the meantime, 'this school is crap' and Pete feels 'like crap' and, even if the school were (objectively) to improve, it would still be crap in Pete's eyes because it represents a certain kind of mothering about which he's anxious.

'Teachers don't teach you anything!' he says. 'They stand there telling you not to talk and not to mess about. But what are you supposed to do when the lessons are so boring? They go on at you all the time, like when you're late or you've had an argument or something. "Where's your homework? Why aren't you paying attention? Why are you talking?"'

I listen as his teachers get a prolonged bashing from Pete. The same teachers have told me that Pete has 'self-esteem issues', that he's dyslexic, gives up on things easily and, when things don't go his way, loses his temper. So, over several weeks, we talk about his life now and his life when he was younger. We talk about his family. We make some connections. He tells me a few things that he hasn't necessarily told other people. But it's this *process* of talking and being listened to that's most important because, if Pete has an abiding suspicion that he's not making sense, that whatever he says is either wrong or foolish or 'crap', then that undermines everything – his confidence, his belief in himself.

He goes on: 'You feel like telling the teachers to shut up! Because, whatever you say, they're not interested. They'd rather be talking to the brainy ones.'

I try my best to understand, to confirm that his feelings are – if not justified – at least real. They're *his* feelings. This is important because, separating gradually from its mother (as fifteen-year-old Pete is preparing to separate from school), a baby still depends utterly on that mother for confirmation of a nascent sense of itself. Unless the mother or mothering-figure mirrors back the baby's movements, sounds, facial expressions, then the baby has no way of knowing what it looks like, what it sounds like, whether it's making any sense, whether it's understandable. And if it's not understandable, it's in danger because it won't be fed properly or comforted. Winnicott (1971) describes a baby looking at its mother's face and 'what the baby sees is himself or herself. In other words the mother is looking at the baby and *what she looks like is related to what she sees there*' (p.112). A sense of self, a sense of ourselves as separate beings develops from this first relationship, from these first interactions with the face looking down and responding to us. As Winnicott puts it, 'When I look I am seen, so I exist' (p.114).

Much of what Pete is saying about his teachers sounds as if it could also be said about a kind of mothering. 'I hate it when teachers say you're not trying! How do they know? They don't know anything! They don't understand us!' Pete's teachers are all made to sound like distracted, impatient, accusing mothers; like mothering-figures looking at their babies and *not* understanding, *not* confirming that these babies really do exist and matter. And a baby may well not be understood if the mothering-figure isn't sufficiently attuned to what it's trying to say. If that person has his or her own preoccupations and can't pay attention to the baby, or if he or she actually resents the baby and *won't* pay attention to its cries, then the baby has no way of developing a reliable sense of itself (Gerhardt 2004). Any 'self' is unable to develop while the baby experiences itself as incomprehensible, unimportant and, ultimately, non-existent. I work with many young people who habitually behave as if they are unimportant – eyes down, keeping quiet, accepting anything, content to remain unnoticed and invisible. And I work with others, like Pete, who panic at the prospect of this and resort to shouting, screaming, drawing endless attention to themselves in a desperate attempt to be noticed.

I'm arguing that a baby's sense of self develops out of the relationship with an attuned mothering presence which is why the process of listening and trying to understand young people is so important because it offers the attunement which some young people haven't experienced earlier in their lives.[1] As a result, their sense of themselves, their sense of who they are, has remained confused. A positive sense of one's self ('self-esteem') comes from being understandable and being understood.

If an attuned, mothering, mirroring presence is available, if a baby can therefore become confident of its own existence and take that for granted, then it can start to acknowledge and be interested in the separate existence of other people, adapting and regulating itself appropriately (Fonagy *et al.* 2004). But some young people seem unable to do this – Pete is often mentioned in staffroom conversations as not appearing to give a damn about anyone else. These young people are (understandably) criticised for behaving as if other people don't matter but, deep down, they may still be unsure about whether they themselves matter. Their shows of couldn't-care-less behaviour may mean that, developmentally, a part of them is stuck at a very early age, still trying to make sense of themselves in relation to other people. 'Am I supposed to control other people? Are other people merely extensions of me or are other people the ones really in control? Are they controlling me?' It's hard to find answers to these questions unless someone has spent time with us as babies from the very beginning, allowing us gradually to make sense of who we are, who other people are and how we can co-exist with other people. Adults talk dismissively about young people 'just wanting attention' as if that were the most heinous, shameful crime and as if they themselves weren't partial to a bit of attention from time to time. But young people with 'low self-esteem' may well need a lot of attention because they've never had any. Driving someone like Pete out into the countryside with his peers and getting him to cross a wobbly rope bridge despite his fears will be an achievement but it will take a long time before achievements like this begin to affect his basic sense of himself.

So what Pete has done, in the absence of anyone to pay attention and listen, is to construct what Winnicott (1965) calls a 'false self' or what young people would call an 'image' as a way of dealing with the world. He can hide his basic uncertainty about himself in a flurry of activity – joking and swearing, jumping around – anything to avoid having to be silent or having to think because those things make him anxious and make him feel invisible. In public, he becomes Pete-Who-Doesn't-Care and Pete-Who'll-Do-Anything-For-A-Laugh. When he gets across the wobbly rope bridge, I imagine him bragging, calling himself 'The greatest! The champ! The boss!' while everyone laughs at him. His relief at avoiding humiliation gets channelled into a brief, lunatic dance of satisfaction on the riverbank.

Characteristically, Pete swings between this kind of manic behaviour and a more disconsolate grumpiness, sitting in my counselling room. When a baby is new-born, it's still effectively merged with its mother with no separate sense of itself. It *is* everything, it *is* everywhere and it controls everything (Kohut 1971). Baby Pete's omnipotent fantasy ('I'm the king of the world! I control everything!') is re-enacted on the riverbank while, at the same time, his genuine relief at crossing the wobbly rope bridge is disguised by this caricature of himself as funny and silly. I remember a teacher once complaining to me about a particular student having 'too much bloody self-esteem!'. There's a relationship between Pete's grandiosity at times like these and his feeling of crapness at other times, sitting with me. When Baby Pete senses that he can't control the world (he isn't omnipotent, after all), he panics because then he feels controlled *by* the world and that's frightening. That's when he feels crap. He's either everything or nothing. He can't imagine what it would be like for control to be shared.

Part of my job is to help Adolescent Pete learn to tolerate a *degree* of crapness and a degree of control. He has to learn to share power with other people without becoming so anxious that he reverts to his habitual all-or-nothing, either-you're-in-control-or-I'm-in-control stance. I spend a long time in our counselling sessions, trying to understand, *really* trying to understand.

'How was today, Pete?'

'Crap!'

'Crap...'

'Yeah, we were supposed to be doing basketball but no one turned up to take our lesson.'

'Because they forgot?'

'Probably. Or couldn't be bothered!'

'Something went wrong...'

'Something always goes wrong!'

'Always...'

'Yeah! They always do stuff like that – telling us that we're doing basketball and then they forget or don't have time or they're away on a course or something!'

'And it feels crap...'

'Yeah!'

If this enacts an early mothering, mirroring process and eventually results in Pete feeling better understood, more secure in the knowledge that he exists, seeing himself reflected in my face, hearing himself reflected in my words, then the next stage is for Pete to start to recognise me as a separate person, no longer threatening to his existence merely because we're separate, but benign and perhaps interesting in my own right. Whenever he asks me a question about myself, I answer it as truthfully as possible. And he asks more and more questions, comparing himself, defining himself against me, understanding what we have in common and what's different. If I've been a mothering-figure for Pete, then he's separating now and learning to be his own person. He sees me around school in between our meetings. He knows that I'll say hello to him but won't ask leading questions. He knows that I'm seeing other students for counselling as well and notices me talking to other people in the playgrounds and corridors. (It can be a relief for young people to know that their parents have other interests and friends and are not wholly dependent on their children for happiness.) He knows that his place in my counselling room is secure, that I'm not about to start cancelling his appointments and that I *won't* be surprised or upset when, one day, he tells me that he's had enough.

As I've said, we depend for a positive sense of ourselves (our 'self-esteem') on being understandable and being understood. Our separate existence, our sense of 'self' depends paradoxically on *other* people understanding how we feel and what we want. We're not born with self-esteem. Our genetic inheritance may give us a DNA profile and various predispositions but it doesn't provide us with that positive sense of who we are. So, while individuality is prized by young people ('I don't care what anyone thinks about me!') and is part of the rhetoric of schools ('You've got to live your *own* life and make your *own* decisions!'), young people know how hard it is to be different from one another and how much they secretly long to be the same and feel connected. Meeting with Pete on his own has been a way of establishing a more flexible, relaxed sense of himself, less bound up with 'crap'. Pete is understandable, therefore he exists. The next stage is to test and develop the adaptability and robustness of Pete's self in a social context, a group.

Joining him in that group will be Conor.

CONOR'S ACHE

I dread meeting with Conor. I know that my well-meaning, jaunty overtures will be made to seem patronising and clumsy as he backs away into silence or, at best, a series of monosyllabic replies. After five minutes I'll be wondering how we're going to get through the rest of our session without drying up completely.

Conor is right at the edge of what a secondary school can accommodate. A skinny, small, undernourished, fourteen-year-old boy, he grew up being beaten and locked out of the house by his father. (Conor goes around looking for fights nowadays.) He therefore spent most of his time outdoors with older boys who taught him about drink, drugs and stealing. (Conor has been involved with all these things at school.) He's been arrested several times and currently lives with a foster family who do their best but who are struggling to keep him in school and away from crime.

Although everything I say seems misplaced, deliberate silence isn't an option with Conor. Silence might be seen as the test of an psychoanalyst's mettle, of the ability to contain a client's unspoken or unconscious pain. Conor has plenty of pain but isn't in psychoanalysis. He's merely a boy at school, meeting with the counsellor. He takes no responsibility for being with me. I'm just a better option than doing more reading and writing in another room with a hard-pressed teaching assistant trying to keep him focused.

All the reports in his school file say that Conor 'lacks self-esteem', with the authors hinting that they're hardly surprised, given his life story. I'm not surprised, either. Any positive feelings about himself that Conor may have dared to develop have been well and truly beaten out of him by a father who always made it very plain that his son was a worthless, pathetic, evil, useless little bastard.

I think of silence as Conor's safety blanket, his way of binding himself together, comforting himself. There are other ways of doing this. Other young people use alcohol and drugs to comfort themselves. Conor holds onto silence and it serves him well, disconcerting people like me who might expect him to join in a conversation. His silence stirs in me the very feelings which probably fill Conor – feelings of uselessness, powerlessness, anger, frustration. Protracted silence gives me a taste of the medicine, allowing Conor himself to sit back and feign indifference. His silence tells me exactly how he feels.

I know all this and knowing it ought to be helpful, yet there's still something almost unbearable about sitting with Conor. In spite of his continuing attempts to look threatening, it's the obvious ache of a boy who's never been loved, desperately resisting the kindness of strangers because he's afraid that they'll love him and he won't know how to respond. So he tries to be unloveable because every kindness hurts – every friendly greeting, every sign of interest in him, every attempt by another person to get closer is a reminder of what he can't allow himself to have, of what was taken away from him along with his toys (burned by his father), his sense of mattering, his 'self-esteem'. When I talk to my supervisor, she says that he sounds like Gollum in *The Lord of the Rings*, a creature no one will go near for fear of his ugliness, his pain. Perhaps I shrink from him because I fear those parts of myself.

I make some resolutions. I decide that, when we're together, I'll be truly *with* him, open to him, imagining what he's feeling and responding as honestly I can. I won't protect myself from him. I won't allow the feeling of uselessness that he projects into me to provoke me into retaliating or causing *him* to feel useless. I'll absorb it and know it for what it is. I'll *like* whatever I can find to like in him. I'll hold a variety of possible conversational topics in my head but I'll be open to whatever occurs in our sessions. I'll go slowly. I'll expect to feel that every session has been a partial failure and I'll try not to let these resolutions make me feel as if I'm going into battle!

Young people develop a positive sense of who they are ('self-esteem') by being with other people, by seeing themselves mirrored in others, recognised and understood by others and by comparing themselves with others. This much was clear with Pete. So I'll expect to be a kind of mothering-figure with Conor in the same way as with Pete, anticipating him, listening to him, being interested and responding to him, gently. But the task with Conor will be more primitive than with Pete because it feels as if Conor's self barely exists at all. Far more important than all these kindly skills will be the much more basic need simply to bear Conor's pain, to endure. I'll be like a mother, perhaps, feeling powerless to help but never leaving her screaming, agonised child.

And yet Conor *has* a mother. He tells me about her.

'She used to give me money and, if my dad found out, he'd go mad and have a go at her. And if I'd already spent it, he'd get something that was mine and smash it.'

The matter-of-factness is hard to bear. I say, 'It sounds like your mum cared about you, Conor. What was she like?'

'All right.'

'What else do you remember about her?'

'Used to give me sweets… And fags.'

If his mother has been a positive experience in his life, then I'm trying to bring her into the room with us, bring her back to Conor as we talk. Everything he remembers getting from her was tangible. I ask what he *needed*, although, even as I say it, I feel stupid because I know what the answer will be.

'Nothing!'

To admit to needing anything from her – anything like fun or closeness or time together – would be too painful. We pause.

'She sounds nice.'

He can't say anything. He has no language for these things. As usual, I'm reminded of my task – offering a relationship which doesn't depend on money or sweets or fags. I feel useless and try to remember my resolutions.

But, over the weeks, some interesting things happen. He becomes animated when I ask what kind of father he would be if he had a fourteen-year-old son.

He would *do* things with his son, Conor says. Take him places. Play football with him. And be strict.

I ask how his son would know that he was loved.

'I'd tell him!'

Conor suddenly looks embarrassed. Something positive, something warm-hearted has been revived in him. It may be the memory of a mother who, in her own way, cared for him. It may be an experience of being cared for by his foster parents, by me or by other professionals. But *something* has given Conor this idea of how he would be with a son of his own.

On another occasion I leave a bag of soft toy animals in the room before he comes in. I know that if I produce them at our meeting and suggest we do something with them, he'll resist my suggestion because it'll seem babyish. So I leave the bag on the floor, a few animals spilling out and, sure enough, as he sits down, he sees them and asks what they're for.

I say I carry them around with me sometimes.

He can't resist tipping them out. He picks up a monkey and sits back, stretching its limbs.

I watch. It occurs to me that he has no idea what to do with this monkey. He has no idea how to play. Most of the things that he's doing with the monkey seem vaguely sadistic.

I pick up a furry, brightly-coloured jellyfish and stroke it.

He's never heard of jellyfish.

I say that they get a bad press but they can be very beautiful and it's not their fault if they sting people. I ask how he would feel if he was a jellyfish.

'Happy! Because I'd sting everyone!'

'Everyone would be scared of you, Conor.'

'Good!'

We laugh.

At another of our meetings, we have a protracted conversation about the way his foster family talk together in the kitchen in the evenings and how his foster dad calls out 'I love you!' as his own son, Conor's age, leaves for school in the mornings. I ask what that's like for Conor.

'Don't mind. If that's what they want to do.'

The fact that he doesn't condemn this show of affection is encouraging because it must powerfully remind him of something he's never had. It would be easy for him to dismiss it as unmanly and 'pathetic'. But he doesn't. Instead he tells me about the new, male teaching assistant he's working with who is a 'gay-boy' and 'probably wants to bum me'!

I could slap him down by saying, 'What makes you think you're so attractive then, Conor?', which would be a standard adult response to a standard bit of adolescent homophobia. But I think his remark is less about homophobia and more about *our* relationship. It may well be that the inexperienced teaching assistant was trying hard to be friends and pushed their relationship too far too quickly. It's alerted Conor to unspoken issues in his relationship with me. Is it okay for him to be emotionally intimate with a man? What's the real meaning of a male counsellor's concern? Are counsellors gay? Or would Conor rather not know so that our relationship can continue without becoming self-conscious?

I don't take the homophobic bait. 'He's probably just trying to help you,' I say. 'Probably no big deal.'

Conor says nothing, which I take to mean that, at this stage, he doesn't want to sabotage our relationship by condemning the emotionally charged part of it – the simple intimacy of sitting together and talking.

When I remark one day that he seems to be growing taller, he looks interested. He doesn't know how tall he is.

I suggest we measure him against the wall and he agrees. So, in time-honoured fashion, he stands in his socks with his back to the wall while I put a book on his head and make a small pencil mark on the wall. With a ruler, we calculate his height and, the next time we meet, measure him again. He's grown a fraction and looks genuinely pleased.

We keep doing this whenever we meet, a series of small pencil marks on the wall secretly charting, not only Conor's height, but also – I think – our growing relationship. Tiny, incremental pencil marks on an empty, white wall.

One day I give him a cup of water from a cooler. He drinks it all and then begins to shred the plastic cup as we talk, tearing it in several places from the rim to the base so that, eventually, it resembles a very small octopus or a very large snowflake.

I *could* ask him if he feels shredded himself. But he would look up, embarrassed, and probably throw the cup away. So, instead, I ask what name he would give the cup if it was a sculpture.

'Don't know. It's just a cup!'

'It looks a bit like an octopus to me.'

He understands. 'No, it isn't. It's one of them jellyfish!'

We laugh. He pretends to make the jellyfish attack me and I pretend to be scared. He throws it aside. (Enough playing for one day!)

We continue to meet and I keep my resolutions. He starts telling me stories about what he and his older mates get up to at weekends. These stories consist mainly of people getting beaten up and getting drunk. They're often stories about loyalty, about mates sticking up for each other in fights, about mates promising to kick his dad's head in 'because of what he's done'. They often feature someone who's out of control (drunk or angry or both) and someone else who's protecting that person from harm (getting beaten up or arrested). I'm at pains not to take his stories at face value, not to throw up my hands in horror but to keep punctuating each story by asking how he felt. I'm trying to distinguish between his behaviour and his feelings because it's so easy for him to believe that he *is* his behaviour. Usually he can't answer my question because he doesn't know how he felt. But I persist. I remember to go slowly because I imagine that it's still tempting for him to terminate our relationship at these first, painful signs of connectedness. He's used to being disconnected from other people and he's used to the various parts of 'him' being disconnected from each other. I think that two parts of Conor's self are coming closer together in his stories – the part of the endangered baby and the part of the protective mother – but I don't comment.

We make another pencil mark on the wall.

JADE'S WAY OF ATTACHING

'I taught David Buckland for the first time today and he was terrible!' Elizabeth tells me. 'Confrontational. Loud. Unco-operative. I didn't know what to make of it. We'd never come across each other before and this was only our first lesson!' Elizabeth is a senior teacher who knows all about difficult students and the challenges they throw down at the beginning of a school year. Crestfallen, she wanders off into the September sunshine. 'Ah well!'

I think no more about it but, shortly afterwards, meet another teacher, Ibrahim, who happens to tell me about his first lesson of the year with another student, Jade.

'She was all over the place,' he says, 'refusing to do anything, throwing things about, stopping other people from working and then getting stroppy with me when I spoke to her!' He smiles but seems rattled. 'I've already given her a detention and it was only our first lesson!'

Ibrahim is an experienced and highly effective teacher. The next day, I bump into him again.

'Today was much better!' he says. 'She apologised for yesterday and was fine all through the lesson. We're friends now!'

I'm left wondering about the extent to which conflict like this can be a kind of attachment process for some young people. Ordinary, slow, gradual, cautious, cumulative attachment is, perhaps, too tantalising, too uncertain, so they try a much more direct method – confrontation – which doesn't *look* like attachment at all (quite the opposite) but which actually has the effect of speeding up the attachment process because, at the end of their first lessons, both these students have been able to stay behind and have a personal conversation with their teacher before any of the other students in the class have had that opportunity. Both can perhaps now feel safer, knowing that they've established a relationship – albeit a confrontational one – with their new teacher.

This is very different from Conor's way of approaching relationships – withdrawing into silence and resisting all overtures. Jade has probably learned that, for her, the best form of defence is attack. She protects her fragile, fourteen-year-old self with hostility while that fourteen-year-old self is secretly looking for attachments.

By chance, Jade is referred to me for counselling soon after my conversation with Ibrahim. I'm wary. On the one hand, she's getting me to herself and doesn't have to compete for my attention with twenty-nine other students. So we may not need to begin with a confrontation. But on the other hand, the intimacy of being alone with me *without* twenty-nine others may unsettle her to such an extent that she falls back on her old friend, the confrontation.

The appointment is made through a teacher who tells me that Jade has 'self-esteem issues' and promises that, yes, Jade is very keen to meet with me. This sounds a bit too good to be true. Sometimes it means that the *teacher* is very keen for the student to meet with the counsellor. I prepare myself.

She doesn't arrive.

Feeling foolish, I enter a classroom where students are all getting on with their work. I whisper to the teacher that Jade and I have an appointment. He points me towards a student who, quite unconcerned, is talking to her friend.

I go across, trying to be inconspicuous. 'Jade?'

'Yeah?'

'I'm Nick. We're supposed to be meeting…'

'Was it now? I forgot!' She gets up, gathering her things and calling to her friend, 'Tell her I'll meet her at break by the canteen.' She calls out gleefully to the teacher as we leave, 'See you, sir!'

Outside, I apologise for interrupting the lesson. I say that I hope it wasn't embarrassing but that I understood she wanted to meet with me and, because my diary gets very full, missing this session would have meant not meeting for a fortnight.

'Yeah, no problem.' She refuses my offer of coffee and sits down.

Only if we can make some attachment will I be able to help Jade develop a more positive sense of herself. (The same is true for Conor.) But already she's making it hard. As I run through my introductory spiel about who I am, what counselling is, what confidentiality I can offer and what will happen at the end of our session today, she looks out of the window, apparently bored.

'Does all that make sense, Jade?'

'Yeah. Are you finished now?'

It sounds as if what I've just said is the most obvious, ridiculous stuff she's ever heard in her life. But in order to attach, we have to find a language. She's heard mine and pronounced it fairly meaningless. Now it's my turn to hear hers.

She launches herself, telling me all kinds of 'random' things (her favourite word); things like having sex with an older boy who said that she was the best fuck he'd ever had, like driving around town with another boy who was high on crack, like beating up a girl who was rude to one of her friends, like telling teachers to fuck off.

I'm challenged on all fronts. There's the swearing, the underage and probably risky sex, the drugs, the violence. My guess is that a lot of it is exaggerated for my benefit, partly to see how shockable I am and partly to see whether I'll say nothing and collude or over-react and misunderstand. It may also be that she's telling me important things about herself – that she feels out of control sometimes, that she wants to be treated as a grown-up, that loyalty is important, that relationships with men (men like me?) are exciting and scary.

We're trying to find a language, a way of understanding each other. I say that the things she's told me sound fun but that I imagine they can be difficult at times. I'm hedging my bets, trying to offer an understanding which accounts for things being both positive and negative.

She listens and seems content with what I've said. Then she says, 'You can't actually do anything, though, can you? I mean, counselling can't actually change anything. It's a bit pointless really.'

I think to myself that she probably feels as if *she* can't change things and *she* feels pointless. But all I say is that I can offer her the chance to talk about these things. I *want* to say that, if only she'd trust me, she'd find me helpful. But I don't say this because it's probably precisely the promise she longs for and will therefore attack. Other people will have made these kinds of promises to Jade – made them and then forgotten all about them. She therefore attacks anyone (like Ibrahim) who promises anything. First lessons of the school year are usually full of promises and I imagine that Jade has resolved never to be disappointed, never to be hurt again.

We agree to meet in a fortnight and, sure enough, when the time comes, she doesn't appear. Again I go and find her and again she comes willingly.

There are young people who need to be pursued like this. I have to *demonstrate* my commitment. It's not enough to sit back and interpret her non-appearance as an unconscious attack on me or as an expression of her ambivalence about counselling. It may be both of these things but it's also a test. In effect, she asks, 'How badly do you want to meet with me? Will you give up at the first sign of difficulty? Will you persist if I'm irritating and inconvenient? How will I know whether or not you care about me?'

When we do sit down together, I say that I'm pleased to see her and she needs to remember our appointments. I say that fetching her from a lesson loses us time. In saying this, my intention isn't to shame her but to indicate that I can stick up for myself and am not going to be a doormat, trodden on and controlled by her.

In these ways, I try to understand and bear her anxiety about attachment. One day, she may well sit down and announce, 'I don't want to meet today!' When that day comes and if she insists, I'll have to steer a course between respecting her and respecting me. She may not want to meet with me, I'll say, but I want to meet with her. I can't and won't make her talk, but I may insist on the compromise of a shortened (not an abandoned) session. This is an important compromise because some young people (like Pete and perhaps like Jade) believe that, unless they control other people, other people will control them. Other people become projected, stray parts of the young person which have to be rounded up and captured for fear that the young person's fragile self will somehow go spinning chaotically out of control. When young people feel most exposed – outnumbered, outwitted, in danger of humiliation – they sometimes resort to explosive anger as a desperate way of holding themselves together, preventing an imagined meltdown of the self, a loss of control. In these situations, adults can easily be convinced that the young person is exhibiting *powerful* behaviour. The opposite is usually the case. But the behaviour *is* intended to regain control of the situation. So, in controlling others, a young person like Jade might be seeking to control and organise her own feelings.

One lunchtime, she's standing with her friends in the school car park and sees me coming towards them. She has to decide whether to ignore me, pretending that she feels no attachment, or whether to embarrass me in front of her friends, attacking the attachment that I suspect she's starting to feel.

She chooses the latter option. 'Oi! Nick, you old fucker!'

This *is* embarrassing. Her friends look at me, waiting to see how I'll react as a member of staff in a school where swearing isn't allowed.

As ever, I have to strike a balance. 'I thought that was you, Jade, swearing at me! I thought, who do I know who would want to embarrass me in front of her friends?'

They smile back, relieved. Jade looks relieved as well. Her attempt at a coded kind of intimacy could have backfired badly.

Neither of us has lost face. I ask them what they're doing and hear all about teachers they claim not to like, lessons they don't like, boys they don't like. The awkward moment passes. Our relationship survives.

I mention it, the next time we meet. 'You put me in a difficult position, Jade, because your friends don't know me and I don't know them. They might have expected me to punish you for swearing.'

'Yeah, sorry,' she says and quickly changes the subject, telling me about some teacher who keeps picking on her.

The way she picked on me, I think to myself. Being picked on is a story commonly told by young people who are responsible for a lot of 'picking on' themselves. I remember hearing about Jade picking on Ibrahim in their first lesson together. The behaviour looks and feels like straightforward hostility but is rarely so because many young people live with a harsh voice in their heads, blaming, criticising, belittling, castigating them. Freud (1923) calls this a 'superego'. It's a voice picking on them. The voice is typically internalised from a parent, experienced in the past as being critical of the young person in some way. It may be an *imitation* of that parent, learned as part of growing up, but it may also be a part of the 'self' which emerged at the time of the baby's earliest relationship with its mother – a voice saying, in effect, 'The reason my mother doesn't respond to me in the way I want is because I'm doing everything wrong. I'm actually unloveable. I must be a bad person. I must try even harder to be good.' For most young people, the superego's voice isn't a problem and serves as a necessary balance against their more unrealistic, irresponsible ambitions. But, for some, it's toxic, it's a curse – a voice forever inhibiting and disabling them. Under those circumstances, what some young people do with that critical voice is to pass it on. They *become* the voice in their head, their own superego, and find someone else to pick on, someone else to criticise.

Jade and I will talk about the feeling of being picked on. We may identify its source, possibly someone in her family, and we'll talk about that person. We'll talk about what Jade might feel like saying *back* to her superego; about all the good things in Jade that her superego overlooks; about trying to live up to an ideal sense of herself and about all that her initial hostility towards other people so effectively disguises.

Her need for attachment may be less obvious than Conor's but it's important not to take her at face value. Her hostility merely passes on to others the same hostility that she herself has experienced. It's her way of making a relationship – the only way she knows. And without safe attachments, she remains a fragmented self, searching for those attachments.

Together with Pete and Conor, Jade will be the third member of my group. The three of them will be joined by Grace.

GRACE'S MISSING STORY

A boy lives happily with his mother. He sees his grandparents a lot and has plenty of friends. Life is good. The only trouble is that he's been excluded from school several times because of a series of violent outbursts.

I ask about his dad.

'Never met him. Left before I was born.'

I ask what he knows about his dad.

'Nothing! We never talk about him.'

Next week is the boy's birthday. I encourage him to take the opportunity to ask his mother all about what things were like before and after he was born. What happened to his father?

Every young person constructs a story of who they are – how they came to be and what's happened in their life. If there are gaps in the story, then it's as if there are gaps in the person – places where the self doesn't entirely join up.

I remember meeting with a mother who was concerned about her son's behaviour in school. She and her husband had divorced when their son was two. She told me that, in his bedroom, her son kept all the photo albums from the first two years of his life. 'He's always looking at them,' she said. She said that his behaviour had improved dramatically after she and his father had attended a school parents' evening together for the very first time.

A young person's story has to be joined up and has to make chronological sense. It has to be flexible, taking account of sometimes contradictory information. For example, 'My mum and dad loved each other and now they hate each other' has to be thought about carefully before it can be incorporated into a young person's story in a way that makes some sense. An old story like 'My dad never cared about me' has to assimilate and make sense of new information such as 'My dad obviously cares a lot about my half-brother'. Our ability to make secure attachments to other people depends on the kind of story we're telling ourselves about who we are and where we come from (Holmes 2001). For the boy who knows nothing about his father and for the boy with the photo albums, the missing parts of their stories need filling in so that they can think about themselves and make meaning of their lives. At times, violent behaviour may well be the inchoate expression of a self which still doesn't cohere, which still doesn't make sense, which can't relax because parts of it are missing.

The fourth member of my group, Grace, looks at me anxiously, tugging at her fringe. She's fourteen. When she was three, her parents split up and, unusually, she went to live with her father while her elder sister stayed with their mother. I ask why this happened.

She doesn't know. She had no contact whatsoever with her mother until she was twelve when, out of the blue, her mother phoned to say that she was in hospital and would Grace like to visit.

Grace thought hard about this. Old feelings of anger and resentment towards her mother came back. But she decided to visit and, two weeks later, arrived at the hospital, only to learn that her mother had died half an hour earlier.

Grace is meeting with me at the suggestion of a teacher because of 'self-esteem issues'. I listen to the mixture of things she feels about her visit to the hospital and her mother's death but there's a sense of her describing all these things at arm's length, as if she can't quite allow herself to feel any of them, as if something is blocking her. In the same detached style, she's happy to tell me about her life at the moment but can't manage to say anything about the years between the ages of three and twelve. She can't remember. 'Nothing really happened,' she says. It's as if her autobiography has a huge hole in the middle and, until that hole is adequately filled, her 'self-history' (Stern 1985) will be limited, her sense of herself incomplete and any real 'self-esteem' therefore impossible.

Holmes (2001) describes a therapist as being an 'assistant autobiographer'. I talk with many young people like Grace about how their parents met, how they themselves came to be born, how they got their names, what was going on when they were babies. We explore the very beginning of their story because that part has often been narrowed to a few basic facts which leave all sorts of emerging adolescent questions unanswered: 'Was I born out of love? Was I an accident? Was I wanted? Was it my fault that my parents split up? Was it because I cried too much?'

Grace's unanswered questions centre on herself at three years old: 'Why did I go to live with my dad? Didn't my mother love me? Was I bad? Was I too naughty? Was my mother a bad person? Couldn't she cope? Did my dad really want me or was he forced to take me?' Until she begins to address these questions, the following nine years will continue to seem blank and uninteresting because Grace has no way of thinking about them. Whatever may have happened during that time will stay as a succession of jumbled-up, meaningless events.

My questions have to avoid letting her answer, 'I don't know'. It's true that she *doesn't* know but together we have to make that not-knowingness more interesting and more varied with all sorts of possible meanings available for Grace to be thinking about from now on.

I ask about her earliest memory but, before she can say 'I don't know', I give her lots of possibilities – food, toys, Christmases, birthdays, grandparents, her sister, holidays.

She says she remembers her sister pushing her out of the pram. I ask what happened. But, of course, she doesn't know. I wonder if her sister was jealous.

'Probably!'

'Because she thought you were the favourite?'

'Maybe.'

'Because you were the youngest and your mum and dad loved you?'

She shakes her head. 'Doubt it!'

'Because she was used to getting her own way? How much older is she?'

'Three years.'

'So for three years she was your mum and dad's only child and then they decided to have you. I can imagine she might have been jealous!'

Grace remembers, smiling. 'She went round telling everyone that she was going to be a sister!'

'She was looking forward to you being born...?'

'Suppose so.'

'She loved you *and* she was jealous of you...?'

I have to stop myself jumping ahead and making some excited therapist's remark about people having mixed feelings about each other. Grace's mum may well have had all sorts of mixed feelings about Grace going to live with her father but that possibility will have to emerge more gradually.

I ask about where they lived and, again, before she can say 'I don't know', I offer possibilities to jog her memory. A flat? A big house? In a village? A town? A nice place? A room of her own? Near to her grandparents? Near other relatives?

She says she thinks they lived in an army house because her dad was in the army.

I ask more about that and whether his work took him away from home a lot, whether her mum worked, whether her sister went to school. From every cluster of questions, one piece of story typically emerges. Her dad didn't like his job. They didn't have much money. Her mum's sister lived a long way away.

As bits of story slowly emerge, we wonder about all sorts of things – how her mum felt, what it was like for her dad, whether her mum and dad each had friends of their own. I offer these thoughts, not as questions to Grace, but as wonderings, not expecting or inviting her to respond but leaving them as possibilities in mid-air. I wonder aloud about how people change and how relationships change, about what it's like, living without much money, about feeling frustrated with life, about whether it's better to stay together unhappily or to part, about how hard it might be to leave your daughter, about some fathers fighting for custody of their children, about children sometimes feeling that things are their fault.

From time to time she comments as an idea stirs. She also does a lot of nodding, as if to confirm that, yes, these are interesting thoughts. They are, of course, thoughts designed to open up rather than close down the possibilities for Grace – thoughts in which she knows I have no vested interest because I'm not trying to convince her of anything. Holmes (2001) writes, 'To tell a story about oneself in relation to others, one has to be able to reflect on oneself – to see oneself, potentially at least, from the outside' (p.69).

She seems pleased. 'I haven't really talked to anyone about this before.'

We agree to meet again and, when we do, we continue the process, gently teasing away at what she knows, what she's pieced together, what she suspects, what she can imagine and what might have been the case. Whenever I sense the story narrowing, whenever she starts using words like 'definitely' or 'always' or 'never', I wonder aloud about whether her mother was *definitely* selfish, whether she *always* did whatever she wanted, whether she *never* really cared about Grace.

The old, fixed story of what happened when Grace was three and went to live with her dad is opening up to new possibilities. Grace is becoming more animated, less detached, more 'herself' as possibilities emerge out of the reflective relationship between us.

She and Jade will join Pete and Conor in the group with a third girl, Allie.

ALLIE'S BEST FRIEND

At her mother's suggestion, Allie has agreed to meet with me. Apparently she's been slipping behind with her school work since breaking up with her best friend a few weeks ago.

'It sounds upsetting,' I say to her. 'You and Gemma had been friends for such a long time. It must hurt.'

She fights with herself, trying not to cry.

Allie's world has changed. Everyone agrees that her self-esteem has taken a battering. Piecing the story together, I gather that she and Gemma met in the first year of secondary school. They did everything together, sharing opinions, holidays, clothes, music, homework. Gemma became, in effect, an extension of Allie – attractive, fun and outgoing – qualities without which Allie felt herself to be ugly, boring and unlikeable.[2]

And then one day, after nearly four years of friendship, it all changed. They argued for the first time and had no way of resolving their argument. The hurt was deeply felt on both sides. Gemma went off with other people (probably because her relationship with Allie had become stultifying), leaving her old friend behind, alone and devastated.

Allie cried and cried. She raged. She wouldn't leave the house. She wouldn't go to school or see anyone. It was as if part of her had died, as if the person she was no longer existed. 'She's just not herself!' her mother says to me on the phone.

Of course, there's always pre-emptive work to be done with best friends like Allie and Gemma, helping them to separate gradually *before* the inevitable catastrophe because it can take a long time to repair a young person's confidence after something like this has happened. It's been very painful for Allie and her family and, for some young people, it's an experience from which they *don't* altogether recover. Allie has retreated. She won't say anything to anyone.

Kohut's (1971) notion of the 'selfobject' is helpful in relation to Allie. Kohut suggests that we have no central, innate 'self' but look for ourselves, look to complete ourselves in other people and in other things. *Who we are* is actually a collection of relationships with a world physically outside our bodies.

He argues that our first selfobject is our mother, with whom we are merged as one undifferentiated self in a calm, mutually admiring relationship (hence his merging of the words 'self' and 'object'). Our mother is who we are. Our mother is all there is. Merged in this way, baby and mother are mutually recognised, mutually understood. Fonagy *et al.* (2004) argue that this is where our original 'self-esteem' comes from: we are omnipotent and wonderful because we believe we are *everything*.

If things go smoothly, we slowly learn to distinguish ourselves from our mothers, a little at a time, once we're ready, once our residual sense of ourselves is strong enough to cope with the fact that she is sometimes at odds with us, isn't entirely controlled by us and may well not be a part of us at all. As these realisations occur, we learn that this new experience of being a separate self, a separate person is tolerable. We won't be destroyed because we've already absorbed from our mothers a strong enough sense of being intrinsically loveable, likeable, interesting and worthwhile.

A baby who hasn't absorbed this (or hasn't absorbed enough of it) will be frightened, will feel incomplete and will look elsewhere to replace an errant or distracted mother with an alternative selfobject to bolster and complete its sense of being a whole person.

When this happens, Kohut describes a second kind of selfobject: a selfobject we idealise and with whom we *want* to be merged. Gemma may have become that kind of selfobject for Allie, a best friend who represented – indeed, who *was* – Allie's confidence. Wolf (1988) points out that it's our *experience* of the selfobject that matters rather than the selfobject itself. For Allie, it's her experience of Gemma, her relationship with Gemma that matters rather than Gemma herself. A family dog, for example, might actually *be* a young person's sense of being loved, so that when the dog goes missing or dies, the young person is understandably distraught. A motorbike might *be* another young person's independence or physical prowess or sexual confidence: 'I can't wait to get my bike!' When any of these things are taken away, it can feel as if part of the young person has disappeared or died. The 'self' is no longer whole, no longer contained. The person is changed.

Young people like Allie invariably end up being described as having 'low self-esteem' because, in Kohut's terms, Gemma had become Allie's selfobject, a part of Allie which went away one day and wouldn't come back, leaving Allie incomplete, grief-stricken, a self uncertain, a self without esteem. I know nothing about Allie's early life but it seems that Gemma became a necessary part of eleven-year-old Allie and, eventually, Gemma outgrew this. She wouldn't be controlled by Allie. She insisted on being herself and no longer an extension of her friend.

This is different from the idea of projection. When we project ourselves onto others, we merely see ourselves reflected in them and feel drawn to or repulsed by whatever we see. Gemma may have been drawn to *Allie* when they first met simply because she saw herself in Allie – another girl lost in a big school and looking for a friend. For Gemma, it may have been a much more straightforward relationship.

A selfobject is also different from Winnicott's (1975) idea of a transitional object. We hold onto a transitional object to ease our separation from an important attachment-figure as we venture forth into the world. A transitional object such as a piece of blanket or a favourite teddy bear comforts and keeps us company. It isn't a part of who we are, whereas selfobjects – be they friends like Gemma, beloved dogs or shining motorbikes – are things we experience as parts of our self and expect to control, Kohut (1971) writes, in the same way that we expect to control our own bodies and minds (pp.26–7).

For Allie, Gemma was more than a transitional object, more than a transitional relationship. I ask what things were like before they met.

'I can't remember.'

Young people often tell me that they can't remember things and I believe them. They forget things that are painful or difficult and they do so in order to survive. But the memories are stored and are usually retrievable, so I ask Allie about simple things like where she lived, what the house was like, whether she had any pets, what primary school was like, whether she went on holidays.

'The first holiday I remember was when my gran was alive and we went to Weymouth.' She remembers a few snippets – seagulls trying to steal her chips, her eldest brother getting drunk and being sick on the pier. I ask about her gran.

'She was nice. She taught me to knit. She used to listen to me read. She used to tell my mum that my brothers were spoilt.'

As we talk, a picture emerges of a grandmother loving Allie, sticking up for Allie, seeing good things in Allie which the rest of the family overlooked. If Allie's mother was preoccupied with her older siblings and if Allie's father was more interested in boys, it may well have been that Allie – the youngest – replaced these parents with an alternative selfobject, a grandmother who could be the part of Allie which was still unformed, unfinished – her confident, clever, outgoing self.

Many young people who ostensibly come to see me because of something to do with 'self-esteem' end up talking about the losses in their lives. They remember being self-confident and enthusiastic before the important event that happened; before a younger sibling was born or before they moved to another town, before their mum and dad split up, before they started getting bullied. The difference between life before and life after The Event was dramatic, they say – not just confusing or upsetting, but something which actually *changed* them. A part of themselves was so identified with whatever was lost that it feels now as if that part has died or been amputated. We work together to find out more about what was lost in order to revive its memory – a sense of specialness, perhaps, before a rival sibling's birth, of playfulness before the family moved to the strange town, of confidence before mum and dad started fighting, of being happy before the bullying started. For Allie, the lost part might be the sense of being valued by someone before her gran's death and before Gemma went off 'with all those bitches'.

'When my gran died, no one told me. Dad said he didn't think I'd be bothered and my mum said she didn't want to upset me. I wasn't even allowed to go to the funeral.'

I listen to Allie's indignation.

'I went to see her grave and I put some flowers on it but it didn't seem like she was really there. It was like she'd gone.'

'Like she'd left you?'

'Like she just wasn't there any more. Like she'd never existed.'

'But she existed in your heart?'

Allie nods.

'And you existed in her heart?'

She looks unsure. I encourage her to tell me more stories about her gran and she does, fondly.

Eventually I ask, 'I wonder what your gran would say now if she knew how upset and angry you'd been feeling?'

'She'd probably tell them all to get stuffed!' Allie says with a smile. 'Probably tell them to fuck off!'

'She probably would,' I confirm, 'because she loved you and knew what you were like.'

Allie nods again.

'I imagine she loved you, Allie, because you were clever and fun to be with. And because you were kind to people and tried your best.'

She nods emphatically, a tear welling in her eye.

We carry on talking. My aim is to help her retrieve the memory of her selfobject, her gran, by remembering the old times and reviving those times *now* through the happy and sad stories, the memories coming back. If we can enjoy and celebrate those stories about her gran, they can be restored to Allie as lost parts of her self to be re-integrated. Some young people seem able to adjust quickly to a loss. But others 'lacking self-esteem' are often the ones who can't adjust so readily which is why, like Allie, they can seem so dispirited and unsure, so incomplete.

We continue to meet. As the weeks go by, her clothes start to change, her taste in music changes, she does different things at the weekends. Eventually, she returns to her peer group, a changed person. She tells me about Gemma and Gemma's new friends. 'I don't go round with that lot any more. I'm not into that sort of thing. To be honest, I don't know what I ever saw in her!'

I can hear her gran in Allie, telling them all to get stuffed.

LEDLEY'S GREATEST FIGHTS

Ledley will join Allie and the others as the sixth member of the group.

He's fifteen – bored with himself, bored with the person he's become. 'People just expect me to fight all the time,' he says, 'and I don't want to do that any more.'

Nevertheless, he's keen to tell me in glorious detail about a fight a few days ago when, despite being massively outnumbered, he and his friends managed to get the better of their much older and bigger attackers. The attackers ran off. 'But they'll be back and there'll be even more of them because everyone around here hates us!' he says proudly. 'They all want to beat us up. But they know what they'll get if they try anything!'

I've heard this story many times before, not only from Ledley but from umpteen boys forever throwing their enemies across car parks and alleyways before turning to face the fresh, oncoming hordes. They all tell the same story, nonchalant about their supernatural strength, but insistent, as if I hadn't fully realised just how ferocious they could be.

I smile back, trying not to laugh, trying not to be bored. 'But you were saying that you don't want to be like that any more, Ledley?'

'Yeah, well, I don't,' he says, 'but if they come at me, I'm hardly going to walk off, am I?'

He's held in considerable esteem by his peers as a fighter. From what I gather, no one is more easily provoked or more ruthless. The reputation he's built for himself has all sorts of benefits. Other young people are keen to be his friend and do his bidding. He's protected from insults and belittlement and even some professionals are wary of him. His bravado suggests that Ledley must be as tough as he looks.

From our conversations, I sense that Ledley the Fighter may be the externalisation of an internal fight Ledley is having with himself – fighting his own need to feel loved, fighting his need for a father, fighting the hurt he's felt in his life. Perhaps the Fighter inflicts on others the cruelty and humiliation Ledley himself has felt. Kohut and Wolf (1978) argue that grandiosity protects against 'disintegration anxiety': the fear that our selves will break down one day; that we'll lose control and become baby-like again. I think young people dread this happening but, at the same time, part of them longs to retreat from the world. They vacillate sometimes, unwilling to go forwards (to 'grow up') but unable to go backwards. Blos (1962) describes adolescence as a second individuation process – a process of separating from family ties and dependencies parallel to the process whereby a toddler separates from its mother. I think it's helpful to understand (but not treat!) young people as big toddlers experiencing the same anxieties as small toddlers. If they can hold themselves together with silence like Conor or with heroic deeds like Ledley, then surely nothing bad can happen? Perhaps Ledley's fighting is another version of Jade's way of attaching through rows – a way of controlling the world before it controls him.

I think he's stuck – afraid to jettison his simple Fighter self because of the security and social kudos that goes with it, but bored because The Fighter is so constraining, because it's become the *only* way he's allowed to be. In a sense, his 'self-esteem' depends on one thing, and so, were he ever to *lose* a fight...

'If you didn't fight, Ledley... If fighting didn't exist, what would your life be like?'

'There wouldn't be anything.'

He has a history, of course. Ledley's fight stories usually involve loyalty and disloyalty and he knows all about these things. His father left when he was two. His mother moved in with his father's best friend whom Ledley still calls dad. That man left and another man moved in with his mum. Ledley's father came out of prison at some point and started a new family. And so it goes on... Promises made, promises betrayed.

I wonder whether fighting has replaced his father and become a kind of selfobject for Ledley. Fighting is male. Fighting is strong. Fighting gives Ledley an identity. Perhaps fighting gives Ledley such an exaggeratedly masculine identity that his need for a father is entirely hidden. Storr (1960) writes that 'Aggressiveness is at its maximum when dependence...is at its maximum' (p.56). Perhaps Ledley tells me about his fights in the same way that a son might bring trophies home to show his father. Perhaps I should congratulate him on these muscular, filial achievements.

Interestingly, he not only fights loyally for his friends ('I could never let a mate down!') but there are other people he's typically drawn to defending – his mother, his baby half-brother and a disabled boy he tells me about one day.

'I hate it when people are ignorant,' he says. 'I saw this boy on holiday, right? He was in a wheelchair and he was, you know, *different*. And near to where we were standing, there were these kids, all taking the piss.'

I gear myself up for one of his best massacre stories – dozens of enemies all biting the dust under the weight of Ledley's blows.

'I told them to shut up.'

'Good for you, Ledley. What happened?'

'Nothing. They shut up.'

'That must have felt good.'

'Not really. I felt sorry for the kid in the wheelchair, that's all.'

I say nothing. Ledley is testing. If I shower him with praise for *not* fighting, he'll retreat into some old fight story because he's scared of seeming soft. So I have to let his kid-in-a-wheelchair story rest. I have to allow it as a normal part of his repertoire, not draw attention to it and risk embarrassing him with dollops of praise for behaving differently.

I ask about Karina, his girlfriend. He mentioned her for the first time a few weeks ago. On that occasion, when I asked what she was like, he said, 'She'll do!' I resisted the temptation to preach about women not being sex-objects and why saying 'She'll do!' was offensive. It was enough that he was telling me about a girlfriend and not about a switchblade.

This time he says that she's a good shag and can I get him some condoms. I ask what she's like as a person.

'All right.'

This much is progress. Slow progress. 'All right' is marginally better than 'She'll do'. Boys like Ledley, moving away from the grandiosity of fights and themselves as warriors often move on to sexual grandiosity and themselves as studs. Suddenly, they tell of huge penises, multiple orgasms, litres of semen and of their girlfriends' eternal gratitude for such wondrous offerings.

Perhaps sex, like fighting, is another way of resisting the threat of disintegration. Ledley the Warrior is giving way to Ledley the Lover but this is new territory and his self-confidence is precarious. Grandiosity attempts a cover-up. I don't challenge him. I don't say, 'I doubt if they *all* fancy you, Ledley!' or 'I'm sure your dick isn't *really* that big!' Instead, I wait. Wait for him to relax. Wait for the grandiosity to lessen as he discovers that I'm not about to expose him. When the going gets tough, some young people fall back on grandiosity because it makes life simpler, recalling an earlier time when, as babies, they believed that they really did control the world and that other people were merely narcissistic extensions of themselves, a time when 'His Majesty the Baby' (Freud 1914) presided over the world. Grandiosity is a comforting but anxious fantasy. So I wait.

Weeks later, he tells me about how much he likes Karina's family and, at last, we're in business.

'It's good the way they do things together. Like, they have meals. They discuss stuff and you can talk to them.'

'That must feel good.'

'Feels like I'm part of the family. Even though I'm not.'

He's obviously loving this alternative family and, so far in the session, there's been no mention of fantastic fights or superhuman sex.

'They must like you, Ledley.'

'Something like that,' he says. 'I really respect Karina's mum. She's brilliant. She said I was good for Karina.'

'Her mum probably realises that you're a nice guy...'

'Naturally!' He tries to deflect my remark.

'She probably realises that you're kind and friendly and good fun...'

'Yeah, yeah!'

I'm pushing my luck. I say no more so that he doesn't have to sabotage what we've already said. We do a quick bit of blokey-football-talk as a way of bringing the session safely to an end, giving him back his defences.

For boys who have separated from their mothers – in many cases prematurely, Sayers (1998) argues – and adopted a position of grandiose, invincible independence, the hardest thing is to re-connect with others and acknowledge things in common with other people. The fear of losing that hard-won independence is great but so is the fear of never being close to anyone again, the fear of loneliness. Fonagy *et al.* (2004) write that, 'The challenge to identity in adolescence comes from accepting not difference, but similarity' (p.321). Having a girlfriend is a socially acceptable way of connecting with someone, acknowledging things in common ('We love each other!') and lessening the isolation. I have no idea how long Ledley's relationship with Karina will last and, in a way, it doesn't matter. For now, he's allowing himself to be appreciated for more than fighting and for more than sex. He's risking other, gentler parts of himself in public and finding that they're acceptable, at least to me and to Karina's family. The possibilities for *who he is* and *who he can be* are expanding. I imagine that, in future sessions, we might move on to talk about his real feelings for Karina but, for now, a little is a lot.

Time to get him into a group with Pete, Conor, Jade, Grace and Allie. In a group, they can all potentially develop a 'self' which is more flexible and robust than a relationship with one other person alone will allow.

FIRST SESSION

There's a chair with sharp, wooden arms and there's a poster on the wall of Homer Simpson with penis and testicles added in biro. I swap the chair for one without arms and take down the defaced poster, cursing whoever spoilt it. Now all the chairs in the circle are identical and equidistant. No one can get hurt on any wooden arms and no one can be distracted by Homer's appendages. The room is as prepared as it can be. My hope is that a calmly organised room will make for a calmly organised group.

I'm waiting for Pete, Conor, Jade, Grace, Allie and Ledley and I'm nervous. It's our first session as a group. I'm pretty sure about what we're going to do and I have various strategies in my head in case things go wrong. But still I'm nervous. I've run dozens of groups with young people over the years, usually with pre-existing groups containing a few potentially difficult young people together with a majority of solid, reliable citizens. I prefer these groups because they're *normal*. They haven't been hand-picked. I've had some tough experiences with hand-picked groups, usually the ten most difficult students in a school, rounded up for a bit of magic wand treatment. I go ahead with the group in order to earn my credibility in that particular school, not because I'm necessarily optimistic about the work. The difference with this hand-picked group is that I already know the six young people because I've been meeting with them individually. I've had the chance to talk with them about the group and they've each agreed to join, albeit with lots of mixed feelings because young people *do* have mixed feelings about groups. Some of their best and worst experiences will always have been in groups. Groups offer the possibility of being liked and accepted but also the possibility of being persecuted and rejected. These young people may all have chosen this group, they may all know me but they don't necessarily know each other and they don't necessarily get on with each other.

I wonder whether my nerves are their nerves. I wonder whether, unconsciously, they're already getting me to feel their feelings for them.[3] If I'm right about this and they're also feeling nervous about the group, I wonder what, under the circumstances, they'll need from me when they arrive and what they'll be hoping that the session will be like.

Structure, I keep telling myself. If I was one of them, I'd be needing the group to be very structured so that I'd know what to do, so that I wouldn't make a fool of myself or say anything stupid. I'd be needing the session to be calm. I'd be needing to know that I was noticed and liked by the person leading it. If I was Pete, I'd probably hide my nervousness behind a mask of negativity. I'd be inclined to say that the group was 'crap'. If I was Conor, I'd hide behind silence and stay very withdrawn. If I was Jade, I'd challenge the group (and especially the leader) at every turn in order to make a connection and feel safe. If I was Grace, I might find it hard to trust the leader. If I was Allie, I'd be wary of getting close to anyone. If I was Ledley, I'd need the two other boys in the group to respect me but, most of all, I'd need the group leader really to *be* the leader, so that I wouldn't have to take over and run things myself.

Someone's coming. I sit in the circle of chairs, facing the door, ready with my most relaxed, attentive greeting.

Pete comes in and immediately asks to go to the toilet. It's the first boundary challenge but these are Pete's nerves speaking. I tell him to leave his bag with me and go to the toilet quickly. He disappears.

Grace and Allie come in together, already an alliance. They sit opposite me, looking around, getting used to the surroundings.

They're followed by Jade who asks if she can leave before the end of the session because she absolutely *has* to see a particular teacher or she'll get into trouble. This is the second boundary challenge and is more serious because it's in front of Grace and Allie. They watch to see how I'll react to Jade.

But, again, these are Jade's nerves talking. This is Jade's ambivalence about the group, Jade's uncertainty about sharing me with the others. I tell her that staying to the end of the session is important and that I'll write her a note to give to the teacher so that she doesn't get into any trouble.

She seems content. I wonder if she's asking whether I really want *her* in the group and whether I *really* want her in the group.

We're waiting for the boys, chatting about the sort of morning that Grace, Allie and Jade have had so far.

Conor comes in. In order not to sit next to me, he's obliged to sit next to one of the girls. He sits next to Grace but pulls his chair backwards, out of the circle.

Pete comes back from the toilet, followed by Ledley. They're obliged to sit in the empty chairs on either side of me.

Ledley notices Conor and sneers, 'What's he doing here?'

He knew perfectly well that Conor was going to be in the group. But, again, these are Ledley's nerves. Putting down another boy is his way of establishing himself. But, unfortunately, Conor will be looking for any excuse to leave the group, so somehow I have to protect him without over-reacting to Ledley's rudeness.

Conor is doing his best to look bored. I say that I'm glad to see everyone and that today we'll be doing some fun things and some serious things. As I talk, I motion Conor to bring his chair back into the circle because it's vital that we begin together. The circle of chairs represents that togetherness and Conor's chair is conspicuously apart. Somehow I have to get him back into the circle without embarrassing him or adding to the hurt he'll still be feeling from Ledley's remark.

I'm repeating stuff that I've said to each of them in private. I *haven't* talked to any of them about 'self-esteem' because that's far too vague a concept. To say, 'this group will help your self-esteem' would be meaningless and would risk making these young people sound inadequate or sound like 'losers' in some way. Instead I've said that the group will be a chance to have some fun and be serious, that it'll be very organised, that it'll be a chance to get to know other people differently and that it will *not* involve any reading, writing or homework. I've explained that we only have four sessions as a group because that's all we've been permitted by the school. I've said that they don't have to be in the group, that they can choose to go to normal lessons instead, that they can always leave the group if they can't bear it but that they won't be able to re-join or join late. This has been enough to persuade each person to give the group a try, with the clincher being the prospect of missing normal lessons.

I start to explain the first exercise, aware that Conor's chair is still pulled back from the circle. Pete, sitting next to me, must begin. He must say his own name, the name of his hero or heroine and one reason why he admires that person. Conor, sitting next to Pete, must then say Pete's name and the name of Pete's hero. He must continue and say his own name, the name of his own hero and one reason why he admires that person. I stop to explain what I mean by a hero or heroine and I give examples. Grace, sitting next to Conor, must then say Pete's name and hero, Conor's name and hero and then her own name, hero or heroine and the reason why she admires that person. The last two people in the circle, Ledley and myself, will have the hardest jobs, I say, because we'll have to remember everyone's names and the name of everyone's heroes. Privately, I hope that this small challenge will appeal to Ledley.

Again, I motion Conor to move his chair into the circle.

Nothing happens.

Jade says that she can't think of anyone she admires. I encourage her to keep thinking.

We have to get started but Conor's chair has to re-enter the circle first. 'Let's begin,' I say. 'Just bring your chair into the circle with the rest of us, Conor.'

Conor still hasn't decided how to react to Ledley's original rudeness. 'Why?'

'So that we can get started,' I say. 'We need you in the circle so that we can begin.' I'm trying to sound as brisk and light-hearted as possible.

To my relief, he pulls his chair forward and we're able to begin with Pete saying his name and saying that his hero is the famous model, Jordan, 'Because she's got big tits!'

Another boundary challenge! There are three girls, three boys and one man in this group. The males outnumber the females and have ended up sitting opposite the females. Is it going to be okay to talk about women having big tits? I decide not to start moralising on behalf of the girls at this stage but to hear Pete's choice of hero as an acknowledgement on behalf of the group that, yes, we are male and female and, yes, some of us have 'tits' and some of us don't. Pete's choice of hero may be a coded attack on the girls or it may be a way of Pete anxiously stating his heterosexual credentials. I decide to wait and see but, if another attack is made on the girls, I'll have to intervene or the group will lose faith in its leader and feel unsafe. Structure, structure...

Bashfully, Conor goes next. 'That's Pete whose hero is Jordan,' he says, 'and my name's Conor and my hero is Muhammad Ali because he was the greatest!'

Conor probably wants to suggest something of his own credentials as a fighter by way of response to Ledley's original challenge. This may be his oblique way of saying, 'Be careful, Ledley, because I'll fight you if I have to!'

Grace begins, 'That's Pete whose hero is Jordan. That's Conor whose hero is Muhammad Ali and I'm Grace and my hero is my dad because he's always stuck by me.'

We work our way round the group until it's my turn. 'That's Pete whose hero is Jordan. That's Conor whose hero is Muhammad Ali. That's Grace whose hero is her dad. That's Allie whose hero is Jimi Hendrix. That's Jade whose hero is her dog, Bella. That's Ledley whose hero is his girlfriend, Karina, and I'm Nick and my hero is Robin Hood because he stole from the rich and gave to the poor and because he was popular and I've always wanted to be popular.'

I squirm but have to model a degree of honesty. I choose 'I've always wanted to be popular' partly because it's true and partly because I imagine that every member of the group secretly wants to be popular. In this first session of the group we're establishing a language, we're establishing norms. We'll quickly go on to our next exercise where people will dash about swapping chairs using the names of their heroes but this first exercise has performed various functions. Through repetition, we've learned everyone's names. Symbolically, there's been a gradual gathering in of the group as each person's name has been added. There's been the opportunity for each person to share something about themselves (their hero or heroine) whilst keeping that information as personal or impersonal as they wish. 'My hero is my dad because he's always been there for me' seems much more personal than 'Jordan because she's got big tits', although Pete was probably saying far more about himself than he realised at the time.

The other effect of this exercise is that everyone has been recognised. Honneth (1995) describes self-esteem developing, not necessarily through other people's approval, but through *recognition*. He argues that self-esteem develops when our needs are recognised and not shamed. My description of babies and mothers learning to understand each other ('Pete's crap') is a way of describing, in Honneth's terms, babies and mothers learning to recognise each other. He describes three kinds of recognition: the recognition that's expressed through emotional concern and love; recognition expressed through the establishment of mutual rights; and recognition that establishes solidarity, where our values are eventually shared by other people. My aim for this group is that the needs – including the underlying, unexpressed, secret needs – of the six young people will be acknowledged gently and respectfully, that we'll find a way of expressing concern for one another, that we'll establish rules and norms which make the group safe for everyone and that we'll find a way to acknowledge our *shared* concerns, our *shared* anxieties and needs. This is ambitious with only four sessions available but we'll try. So far, we've recognised names;

we've recognised and not shamed the small piece of information about themselves that each person has offered to the group; and we've established a circle of chairs, representing something important about our individual worth and equality as people. Objectively, this may not seem very much but, in my experience, the eventual quality of a group's experience depends very much on the quality of its beginning, in the same way that the development of one person's sense of self depends very much on the quality of that person's first interactions with the mothering, mirroring face looking down, recognising or not recognising the baby lying there. Fonagy *et al.* (2004) describe the way in which this basic experience of being recognised subsequently enables a child to regulate its own behaviour, its own self.

I've promised the group some fun and that's important. But even the 'fun' has to be structured. We do our frantic chair-swapping exercise which everyone enjoys and which arbitrarily breaks up the seating arrangement so that we no longer have the males and females ranged on opposite sides of the circle. Eventually, everyone sits back, panting, surprised, wondering what's coming next.

I explain that each person (including me) is going to have a turn in the spotlight (Conor, Grace and Allie immediately look horrified) but that this is easy because, while they're in the spotlight, they must say nothing. Every other person must think of something about the person in the spotlight that they imagine to be true but don't already know for a fact. I use Allie as an example.

'If Allie was the person in the spotlight, she would just sit there and say nothing. The rest of us have to do the work. We try to imagine things about Allie – where she lives, what she likes doing, what she had for breakfast, how she gets on with her mum, how she feels about school. It's up to you. Each of us takes a turn, going round the circle, and when it's your turn, you say aloud one thing you imagine to be true about Allie but which you don't already know for a fact. Allie listens. And when we've finished going round, she can say as much or as little that's true about herself as she wants. She's not forced to say anything.'

I give them more examples of the sort of things that they might choose to imagine.

Probably afraid that, because I've just used her as an example, she'll now have to go first, Allie says, 'Do we *have* to do this?'

I say that we're all going to have a turn and I ask who would like to be the first person in the spotlight. No one volunteers.

Pete says, 'Make one of the girls go first!'

Jade tells him to get stuffed.

I say that no one is going to be forced by anyone else. I wait.

'Oh, go on then!' says Ledley in his best let's-get-it-over-with-but-secretly-I-can't-wait-to-be-in-the-spotlight voice.

Grace is sitting between me and Ledley. I tell everyone to be imagining things about Ledley and tell Grace to go first. I'll go next, I say, and we'll continue around the circle.

'What if you can't think of anything?' asks Pete, presumably worrying about saying something that might offend Ledley.

I give lots more examples, mixing the superficial with the personal.

Grace begins, 'I imagine you've got a motorbike.'

Ledley looks pleased.

I remind him to keep quiet until everyone has spoken. I say, 'I imagine that you miss not seeing your dad.'

He looks blank.

Allie says, 'I imagine you like fighting.'

Conor says that he can't think of anything.

I tell him to keep thinking and we'll come back to him.

Pete says, 'I imagine you've had sex with Karina.'

Ledley glares at him.

Jade says that she can't really think of anything but that she imagines Ledley spending a lot of time in front of the mirror in the morning.

We go back to Conor, twisting on his chair.

'Don't know. I imagine you smoke.'

Everyone has had a turn and Ledley is keen to get going. 'I don't smoke – you do!' he says to Conor. 'No, I don't spend a lot of time in front of the mirror, Jade. I do fight but only when I have to…' He tries to remember other things that people have said. 'I don't miss seeing my dad because he's a bastard! And I can't think of anything else.'

Pete smirks. 'What about Karina?'

'Pete, do you want to get beaten up?'

I ask if there's anything else that Ledley wants to say.

There isn't.

Grace is next in the spotlight. We go round but I'm forced to intervene when Pete says that he imagines her having sex with lots of boys. I point out that if these are the only things he can imagine about people in the group, then people will imagine the same kind of things about him. I say that I know him and that he's a much more interesting person than that.

This seems enough to reassure Pete who, to be fair, is expressing a particular, unspoken anxiety on behalf of the group as well as himself and has been doing so from the very beginning. It's an anxiety which goes something like: 'We're male and female in this group. If we become intimate, we might start fancying each other because intimacy automatically leads to sex. And what then? Our lack of sexual experience might be exposed. Our seemingly confident, false selves might disintegrate. It's going to be hard for anyone to be honest in this group when we all feel so unconfident about ourselves.'

The first session of any group usually throws up all the issues which the group will subsequently work on. I make a mental note to address the specific issue of sexual anxiety in our second session but the group's broader anxiety about exposure and humiliation will be central to all our work because, for these young people, the fear of fragmentation and disintegration (Kohut 1971), the fear of their fledgling selves breaking down is constant.

Everyone eventually has a turn in the spotlight. Interesting things are imagined (sometimes saying more about the person doing the imagining) and some interesting things are revealed. The exercise is important because it gives everyone a chance to test how much of themselves they can reveal. I've deliberately engineered things so that I'll be the third person in the spotlight and will be able to say things about myself that the group hadn't expected – honest things, more vulnerable things, things about my childhood, things that scare me. I'm hoping that this will give others permission to do the same but the crucial thing will be how our small revelations are received by the other members of the group. Will we be mocked? Will we be ignored? Will we be pressured into saying more or will we be allowed to keep our defences intact? The fear of being exposed is terrible for young people because many of them can remember times – possibly even from birth – when their need was obvious but wasn't understood or recognised. Since then, they've been desperately trying to cover up, to protect themselves from that kind of exposure and vulnerability. To take away Conor's silence or to take away Ledley's grandiosity would be cruel. On the other hand, a safe enough group may eventually allow Conor to *temper* his habitual need for silence and a safe enough group may allow Ledley to *amend* his grandiose behaviour. If Winnicott (1971) is right and we do begin to develop a sense of our selves by looking up at an original mothering, mirroring gaze, then this exercise also has that mirroring function, effectively saying, 'This is how others see me and this is how I see myself.' For most, there will be a difference between the two perceptions and an opportunity to think about the implications of that difference. 'When I see myself as useless, how come other people like me? When I think I come across as confident, how come other people think I'm not really so confident?' Perhaps the mutual recognition of the baby–mother relationship is our first experience of being in a group. A group of seven people like this one might only be an extension of that original experience – a hall of mirrors with six versions of a mother reflecting us back to ourselves.

We do another exercise whereby each person takes a turn to complete the sentence which begins 'One thing I'm *not* is…' without saying anything that anyone else has already said.

I start. 'One thing I'm not is young.'

'One thing I'm not is a bitch!' says Jade.

Inevitably, Pete says, 'One thing I'm not is gay!'

Grace, overweight, says, 'One thing I'm not is thin!'

Allie says, 'I don't go round with any group in school.'

Conor says, 'I'm not here.'

Everyone laughs.

He smiles.

Ledley says, 'I'm not a woman.'

We go round the circle four times, getting lots of these things out into the open before switching to a more difficult sentence which begins 'One thing I *am* is…'

Ledley says, 'I'm a fighter.'

Conor says, 'I am nothing.'

To my relief, Ledley doesn't seize on what Conor has said but merely looks surprised.

Allie says, 'I'm a chocolate-eater!'

Grace says, 'I am fat.'

Again, to my relief, no one comments or tries to convince her otherwise. It's much better for these things to be said and heard and allowed to reverberate. If it's safe enough for Grace to say these things without other people passing comment, it may become safe enough for her to try out more of the things that she hasn't said before.

Pete says, 'I'm a player of computer games.'

Jade says, disarmingly, 'I get angry a lot.'

I contribute statements about myself as well. After two rounds of 'One thing I am' we end with a round of 'One thing I wish'. Still more interesting things are said – things made possible because we began with 'One thing I'm not' which is easier than 'One thing I am' or 'One thing I wish'. Young people usually feel much safer describing what they're *not* than what they are. And feeling safe is crucial in a group like this.

There are eight minutes to go before the session ends. We spend some time discussing rules. Some groups begin with this discussion but, in my experience, young people find it hard to think about what rules they might need to make for themselves until they've got more of an idea about the group itself and what might happen which could require rules. It's also true that, in the beginning, they need the group leader (in this case, me) to take responsibility for enforcing any rules until they themselves are more confident. Giving young people responsibility for regulating their own behaviour is a gradual process. Giving them too much responsibility too soon is frightening, like a parent going off and leaving the baby to look after itself.

We make a rule about confidentiality. Jade suggests another rule about not being rude to each other and the group agrees. Grace says that we shouldn't *have* to say things if we don't want to and, again, the group agrees. All these things are written down on a large sheet of paper which I pin to the wall once graced by Homer Simpson.

This has been a good first session. We end with something deliberately silly, passing an old shoe around the circle, but we're only being able to grip it with our elbows. This is easy. So we pass the shoe around again, this time holding it only between our knees.

Conor and Ledley have ended up sitting next to each other. Ledley stands with the shoe wedged between his knees but the thought of his knees and Conor's knees coming close enough to pass the shoe between them is too much. They drop the shoe.

Pete asks, 'What happens now?'

I explain. 'The people who were *both* responsible for dropping the shoe each have to say one thing that's been good about our session today.'

'That's easy!' Ledley says. 'The chair-swapping thing we did at the beginning!'

Conor says he can't think of anything.

I give him suggestions.

'Yeah, that.'

'What?'

'What you said about getting to know people. That.'

He's off the hook and we move on, passing the old shoe, this time by balancing it on our feet. Nobody drops it. The session ends and they rush off.

Jade doesn't ask for the note for her teacher.

SECOND SESSION

There's an empty chair in the circle. Pete says that Conor isn't in school because he was arrested at the weekend. Nobody in the group seems to know why. Ledley starts moving the empty chair out of the circle. I tell him to leave it where it is.

'Why?'

'Because Conor's still part of our group, even though he's not here.'

'So he won't need his chair, will he?'

This is the first time that Ledley has challenged me in public. In the first session he was preoccupied with Conor. But now that Conor is conveniently out of the way and Pete content to let Ledley have his way, I'm the only male between Ledley and domination of the group. Jade, Allie and Grace might have something to say about that but, in the meantime, this is a confrontation I can't afford to lose, partly for the sake of the group (who don't want to be dominated by Ledley) and partly for the sake of Ledley (who doesn't *actually* want to dominate but does so because that's the way he knows of staying safe in an unfamiliar situation). This group has to offer Ledley an experience of being safe while being looked after by someone else.

'Leave the chair,' I insist. 'We'll pretend it's Conor's chair and we'll keep it for him for next week.'

'What if he doesn't come back?'

'How would you feel about that, Ledley?'

'Wouldn't make any difference to me. I don't care if he's here or not!'

I ask what the others would feel.

No one says anything and I let it rest because, although no one is challenging Ledley, no one is actually supporting him. It would be easy for the group to unite around a dislike of Conor. Silent, stubborn, uncomfortable Conor could be made to represent all their individual awkwardnesses, all their unspoken unhappinesses. His absence could represent a part of them which might also – secretly – have preferred *not* to come to the group today. In attacking, in denigrating the idea of Conor (as Ledley is implicitly inviting them to do), they would unconsciously be hoping to get rid of these uncomfortable parts of themselves. But they haven't. Conor remains invisibly in the group and Ledley doesn't have to run it.

We do an exercise which involves everyone changing places and shouting things out as a large teddy bear is passed around the group. They enjoy this and laugh a lot and we do it several times.

Finally, we sit down again and I draw their attention to the rules we made together the week before, posted on the wall in

Homer Simpson's space. Nobody has anything further to say about these rules because, I suspect, they're meaningless. At this stage, the group doesn't trust itself to police them. The group is still reliant on me to do that, and so, however helpful these rules might be, they're cosmetic.

I explain a new exercise. The chair I'm sitting on is the hot seat and the object of the exercise is to get off the hot seat as quickly as possible. To do that, the person in the hot seat has to tell the group one thing which makes him or her different from anyone else in the group. I give examples. A person might be different simply because of their name or because of where they live, because they have a dog called Lassie, because they were born in Germany, because they hate rice pudding, because they don't get on with their step-mother. If anyone in the group *shares* whatever the hot-seat-person has said, then they must say so because that keeps the hot-seat-person in the chair and he or she must think of something else. But if the difference *is* unique to the hot-seat-person, then everyone moves round one chair and somebody else is obliged to sit in the hot seat.

We begin.

I say that I grew up in Trinidad. 'Did anyone else grow up in Trinidad?'

They look bemused.

Pete asks, 'What's Trinidad?'

I explain.

We all move round one seat.

Grace says, 'My name's Grace.'

We move round again.

Allie says, 'I've seen the house in London where Jimi Hendrix lived.'

We move again.

Ledley says he once ate a snail.

Everyone makes horrified noises.

Pete says he's got a particular kind of bike.

Ledley says he used to have one like that but sold it.

'So Pete's the only person who has that bike now,' I clarify. 'That's a difference. Everyone move round.'

Jade says that she hates a particular teacher. Grace, Allie and Pete all agree. So Jade has to think of something else. She says that she's the only person in the group with asthma.

This is news to me. I ask her to say more and she says that she's had it since she was five and her brother also has it.

Ledley says that his uncle has it and he thinks his grandfather died of it.

Grace says that she once lived next to a little boy who had asthma and she remembers the ambulance coming to get him one time when he had a bad attack.

There's a pause, a silence.

I don't pursue it. This is too soon to open up the conversation. We'll do that once they feel more confident. For now, we move round and I'm in the hot seat again. I say that I don't always feel as confident as I look.

Jade, Allie, Grace and Pete all agree.

I pretend exasperation and have to think of something different and we go on in this way. One of the most powerful threats to any young person's 'self-esteem' is the prospect of being shamed. Shame strips away self-confidence and self-belief (Mollon 2002). Shame mocks, belittles, derides. Young people are regularly shamed for being different from their peers in some way and their anxiety about being different is, therefore, acute. This exercise *rewards* difference because, if you're different, you get to move out of the hot seat. It also establishes implicitly that we're *all* different and that, often, whatever we think makes us different (the potentially shaming thing) is actually shared by others. Jade can reveal that she has asthma and other members of the group immediately have their own asthma stories to tell. I can say, 'I don't always feel as confident as I look,' knowing full well that, if they're honest, most of the other members of the group will admit to that. I *don't* embarrass anyone by asking them to explain why but we simply move on. The cumulative effect of the exercise – and we move round the circle several times – is to make difference acceptable, normal, even interesting. Pete says he's crap at reading and writing. Jade and Grace say that they are as well. Jade says that her father's in prison and Ledley says that his father *used* to be in prison. Grace says she didn't see her mother before she died. Allie says she's got a pair of leather bondage trousers. Ledley says he wants to be a boxing promoter.

They look pleased with themselves.

The next exercise requires everyone to have a name card. I give out blank pieces of card and each person writes his or her name with the big felt pen we pass round the group.

I hold out a pack of statement cards that I've prepared. The first person picks a card from the down-turned pack, reads out what's written on it and places it, face upwards, on the floor in the middle of the circle. That person says what he or she thinks about the statement and places his or her name card on the floor as near to or as far from the statement as he or she agrees or disagrees or has mixed views about the statement. Everyone else then places their name card as near to or as far from the statement as they agree or disagree with it and the person who originally read it out chooses one person to explain why they've put their name card where they have. Other people can then comment before we all pick up our name cards and move on to another statement from the pack.

Jade volunteers to go first. She pulls out a statement card and reads, 'Fighting is pathetic'. 'Yeah, I agree,' she says. 'What do I have to do?'

I ask her to say why she agrees.

'It *is* pathetic,' she says. 'I mean, it doesn't prove anything, does it? Fighting is just silly little boys who think they're hard.'

I ask her to place her name card on the floor. She puts it right on top of the statement in the middle, indicating complete agreement.

I ask the others to place their name cards according to what they think.

Ledley puts his name card by his feet. Pete's is halfway towards the statement in the middle. I'm nearer to the middle while Grace and Allie are in agreement with Jade.

I ask her to choose one person to explain their point of view.

'Ledley!'

He looks embarrassed. 'There's nothing wrong with fighting, is there! Sometimes you *have* to fight if someone's having a go at you. It's natural!'

'Yeah,' Jade says, 'but you fight all the time, Ledley. You *like* fighting!'

'So?' He's got himself into a corner.

I ask what other people think.

Nobody wants to speak. I suspect Pete is reluctant to say anything that might distance him from Ledley even though his own name card is placed halfway towards the statement in the middle. Grace and Allie are keeping quiet.

'What do *you* think?' Jade asks me.

I say something about the importance of fighting for justice and fighting for a belief but not fighting to bully people or to cover up other feelings.

There are vaguely approving noises but, still, no one wants to say any more so we move on quickly, picking up our name cards and starting again with Ledley taking and reading out a statement which says, 'My mum understands me'.

'That's true,' he says. 'Well, she doesn't understand everything about me but we're pretty close. I'd kill anyone who did anything to my mum!'

Ledley has just been challenged by Jade about fighting. He can't threaten her, the way he might threaten a rivalrous boy, so he quickly has to find new ground. He can't be seen to be too close to his mum, so he protects himself with this protestation of blind, murderous loyalty to balance any soft-heartedness he may have betrayed. Amongst young people, loyalty to mothers is a given, something which can't be challenged. It's a safe position. Yet, having spoken, he still puts his name card only halfway towards the statement in the middle and I'm pleased, because for Ledley to experience and admit to having mixed feelings about anything is important.

One of the beauties of this exercise is that everyone expresses an opinion – even if it's a non-verbal opinion – without being shamed. The skill is to prepare a pack of statements that will provoke a range of opinions. This statement could just as easily have read, 'My mum *doesn't* understand me', provided it provoked a spread of name cards on the floor because then a conversation could begin.

On this occasion, the statement works. Pete, emboldened, says that, unlike Ledley's, *his* mother doesn't understand him in the slightest. The three girls also have differing opinions, which they share.

Another aim is to allow the group to talk about its underlying anxieties. So when Allie goes next and reads out a statement saying, 'Boys are only interested in one thing', the ensuing conversation picks up where Pete's attacks on the girls the week before (big tits, Grace allegedly having sex with lots of boys) left off. On the whole, the girls agree with the statement and say so vehemently, while Pete and Ledley are obliged to defend the courtly sensitivities of boys. This is an important conversation for the group to be having (and the exercise is only a structured way of provoking a conversation) because my guess is that, having been able to talk in this way, an *unspoken* anxiety in the group will be allayed and they'll be better able to recognise one another as people, some of whom happen to have 'tits' and some of whom don't. In casual conversation, young people habitually, incessantly tell each other their likes and dislikes, waiting for a response, waiting to see if these parts of themselves are mirrored back by friends. If a particular attitude is shared (or, at least, not condemned), the anxiety lessens. If an attitude is *not* shared but not condemned either, the anxiety lessens nevertheless.

Everyone has a turn to read out and start a conversation about a statement. Grace gets 'My dad is my hero' while Pete gets 'I am popular', which proves to be the cause of much discussion in the group with Allie, in particular, insisting that she's never in her life cared what anyone thinks about her. I get 'Being gay is unnatural', which I deliberately added to the statement pack the night before, guessing that there would be homophobic anxiety lurking in this group as there's been in almost every group I've ever run. To my surprise, Ledley is the person who leads the there's-nothing-wrong-with-it argument while Allie (perhaps recalling the charged intimacy of her old friendship with Gemma) is the person most insistent on heterosexual norms.

As we talk, I notice Pete picking up his name card and absent-mindedly beginning to tear strips off it.

A lot of thoughtful things have been said and a lot of anxieties voiced, implicitly. People haven't been shamed but have had the chance to try out parts of themselves they would otherwise have kept hidden. We end by going round the group once more with everyone completing the sentence, 'One thing that's been good today is…'

Jade says, 'Getting to know people.'

Ledley says, 'Everything.'

Grace says, 'Hearing what everyone has to say', which probably means that she herself has appreciated having the chance to say a few things.

Pete says that the fun exercise at the start was the best.

Allie says, 'I didn't know that we would all get on so well!'

I say that I've appreciated their honesty and, as they get up to go, remind them that, with luck, Conor will be back in the group next week.

Ledley goes out, mumbling something I can't hear.

THIRD SESSION

It's been raining all morning. The entrance mats are sodden and mud is slowly being smeared into the corridors and classrooms. Earlier, I saw Conor in the distance, head down, loping along in wet, flapping trousers.

'Can we do what we did last week?' asks Grace. 'That thing with the teddy bear? That was good!'

The others are coming in, damp and fussed and complaining. I say it's really good to see them all again but we're going to be doing some different things this week. I make a point of welcoming back Conor.

Grace asks him, 'Did you get arrested last week?'

He nods.

'Why?'

''Cause of something I didn't do!'

'What?'

'Just something!'

They're all listening.

'You can tell us,' says Jade, joining in.

'Nothing to tell.'

'Oh well, please yourself!'

Foulkes (1964) argues that, when someone is talking in a group, that person is always talking *for the group* as well as for themselves. In that sense, a conversation has begun about openness and secrecy. In this conversation, Jade is the spokesperson for the group and is effectively saying, 'Tell us about yourself, Conor! Open up!' while another conversation has begun about Conor's absence the week before, with Grace as the spokesperson, effectively saying, 'Tell us about yourself, Conor, the way we told each other things about ourselves last week when you weren't here!' Her enthusiasm for an exercise to be repeated from the week before may be because she enjoyed that exercise but it may also, implicitly, be a way of asking for another session without Conor: 'Please can we have a session like last week when Conor wasn't here?'

In this group of young people, all of whom are classified in reports as having 'self-esteem issues', it's not surprising that openness is an issue. In their different ways, they've all learned to protect themselves from shame, from being unrecognised, from being misunderstood. Our first two sessions together have given them opportunities to share more than they might normally do. That experience has been exciting but also nerve-wracking. They want to do more of it but they're scared to do more of it.

Then Conor returns from a week's absence and, as I know from our individual sessions, habitually protects himself with silence. It's easy for the group to interpret this silence as a *refusal* to enter the group rather than as a particular kind of wary, nervous defence, deployed in the same way that they all have their own defences. And, because there's a nervous part of those who were present for the second session which, of course, would rather *not* have been there and would rather *not* have shared those personal things, it becomes easy to scapegoat Conor as the odd one out, the one who won't join in, the one without whom we'd all feel more comfortable if we could only get rid of him. Mollon (2005) writes that people try to impose an identity on others in an attempt to escape their own sense of incipient fragmentation, their fear of disintegration (p.104). If we can get everyone else in the group to be like us, we'll be safe. Just as a young person with a poorly developed sense of self might use a particular defence or behaviour to avoid breaking down into separate parts, to bind him or herself together, so a group or a gang will often impose an identity on itself in order to avoid its internal differences and potential splits. Instead of being separate individuals who might sometimes disagree with each other, they *all* appear to have the same opinions, attitudes, likes and dislikes. Conor's absence and obvious wariness about committing himself to the group makes the other members uneasy. It's much harder to be confident about being a group if one member is missing or disaffected.

Jade says, 'I thought this group was so that we could talk about stuff?'

I nod.

'Well, he's obviously not prepared to do that, is he?' she says, referring to Conor. 'Why can't you tell us what happened, Conor? We're not going to tell anyone! We've got a rule about not saying what anyone else said!'

'And we've also got a rule,' I remind her, 'that no one has to say anything they don't want to.'

She sits back, embarrassed, pulling an ostentatiously bored face and sulking.

I decide to go ahead and explain the exercise that I'd planned. But this is too much for Jade.

'This group really pisses me off!' she says. 'I don't see why you just let him sit there and say nothing but the rest of us are expected to join in and do these stupid games! It's pathetic! I'm going!' She gets up and walks out.

'She's right!' Allie says. 'There's no point in being here if Conor isn't going to say anything!'

Grace, Pete and Ledley are also clearly on Jade's side.

I insist, 'Conor has a right not to say things.'

'So the rest of us are supposed to do all the talking, are we?' says Ledley indignantly, finally returning to the confrontation between the two of us which simmered briefly during the previous session. Ledley's aware that I'm being challenged and is immediately anxious in case my authority disappears and he has to take over.

I have two main tasks. The first is to survive these attacks without retaliating. If the group is a baby, temporarily afraid and screaming, my task is to hear and attend to it without punishing the baby or being alarmed by its screams. That way, the baby will learn that its fear is bearable, isn't shameful, isn't bad and can be understood. As I've said, self-esteem begins with being understandable and being understood.

Grace wants to go after Jade to see if she's all right.

I tell her to stay. 'Jade's a strong person. She'll be all right and she'll come back when she decides.'

My second task is to find a way of protecting Conor while helping the other members of the group to acknowledge the parts of themselves that he represents. Conor himself is unlikely to leave now. If the group was provoking him to leave in the belief that this would take care of their underlying anxiety, it didn't happen. In that sense, Jade had to leave because Conor didn't and the others might all have walked out with her, leaving me and Conor behind. They are now wholly identified with Jade and I've become the enemy instead of Conor. Suddenly, it's all my fault. I caused Jade to walk out (apparently) and I caused their uneasiness in the first place by convening such a stupid, pathetic group.

I feel stuck (probably feeling their stuckness). I ask what they're feeling.

No one says anything. A collective sulk is going on – a refusal to play this game. The five of them sit staring at walls, chair legs and the floor as if they, too, have walked out.

Ledley mutters, 'This is pathetic!'

'Because I can't make it all right, Ledley?'

'What? What are you on about?' he says, glaring at me. 'This is pathetic because we could be doing something useful, instead of sitting here in a stupid circle with nothing to do!'

I try to explain. 'I think it can be really hard being in a group. It's hard to trust other people and it's hard to say what we really feel sometimes. It's hard to know what other people will think and it's hard to know what other people are feeling… What *are* people feeling?'

'I'm not feeling anything!' Allie says, unconvincingly. 'I just wish we could get on with something!'

'I'm annoyed,' Grace says, 'because I was really enjoying this group last week and I was looking forward to talking about things this week.'

Allie and Pete agree with her. I suggest that we try something and I'm about to explain what I mean when there's the sound of doors slamming and Jade comes back into the room. She sits down, still sulking. I welcome her back and say that I'm pleased she felt able to come back.

'Didn't want to,' she says, 'but the teachers made me. They said I've got to talk to you if I want to leave this group. *Which I do!*'

I keep quiet.

'It's pathetic!' she says. 'I mean, what good is this group doing us? How is this supposed to help us? All we do is talk! And Conor doesn't even say anything!'

'It was good last week when we did that thing with the teddy bear,' Grace says, 'but so far this week it's been rubbish!'

'You've had the guts to say a lot in this group,' I say to Jade, 'like about your asthma and getting angry and your dad in prison. It must be really difficult when it feels as if other people can't always say so much.'

'Yeah,' she agrees, looking pleased.

'I suppose we're all different and some of us don't have as much confidence to say things in case we get laughed at.'

She shrugs. 'Yeah, but I wouldn't laugh at anyone!'

'That's good,' I say, 'but I suppose it takes time for other people to find that out and for people to trust each other. I bet everyone in this group agrees with you about not laughing at other people. But I bet everyone would still be quite nervous about saying personal things.'

I'm hoping that what I've said echoes what the rest of the group is feeling; that by describing their ambivalence in this way, they can bear *both* feelings and not get caught up in a war between I'll-tell-you-everything and I'll-tell-you-nothing.

Something seems to have shifted. There's a pause.

'Can we get on now?' Jade says, huffily.

I describe the exercise I'd been planning to use which, as usual, gives everyone an opportunity to contribute at whatever level they feel safe. 'We'll go round the group,' I explain, 'with each person finishing the sentence which begins, "One thing that irritates me is…" Each person must think of something irritating that's different from what anyone else has already said. And, if you yourself agree with what someone else says, you must click your fingers to show that you agree.' I begin. 'One thing that irritates me is people being late. Anyone agree with that?'

No one clicks their fingers.

Pete, who's due to go next, asks, 'What does "irritates" mean?'

I'm pleased that he's asked and pleased that no one has jeered. Suddenly the group feels very purposeful.

'One thing that irritates me is my little brother,' he says.

Allie and Jade both click their fingers.

'My sister!' Jade clarifies. 'She's really irritating!'

Ledley says that he's irritated by people who are two-faced and we all click our fingers with relish.

Grace says she's irritated by politicians and everyone agrees. Jade is irritated by teachers who break their promises and, again, everyone clicks. Allie is irritated by bad haircuts.

And then it's Conor's turn. 'One thing that irritates me is the police.'

Ledley and Pete click their fingers because saying you hate the police is obligatory. Even Jade, I notice, is tempted to click her fingers in agreement with Conor but stops herself just in time.

Conor has contributed. Honour is satisfied. We begin a second round, finishing the sentence which begins, 'One thing that annoys me is…' with people clapping their hands if they agree. We move from that to a round of 'One thing that angers me is…' with people stamping their agreement and, from that, to a round of 'One thing I hate is…' with people saying 'Yeah!' if they agree.

Lots of things get said – things about families, about friends and enemies, about school. Conor contributes in his own way and there's much agreement in the group about all sorts of things. The usefulness of the exercise is partly this sharing of experience and partly the opportunity to voice lots of individual anger. But safely. Within a structure. Without being judged and without having that anger rationalised away by adults. Self-esteem begins with being understandable and being understood. It doesn't come from being told that one's *feeling* is unjustified or dangerous or wrong. A feeling is a feeling. A thought is something else. Feelings and thoughts come together and learn to co-exist, gradually informing one another as a young person grows up. But if young people's feelings (especially their most inchoate, primal feelings) have never been acknowledged in the first place, it's very difficult for those young people to build a secure sense of who they are, a sense of where they end and others begin, a sense of self gradually incorporating more and more thoughts. Stern (1985) writes that, 'Sense of self is not a cognitive construct. It is an experiential integration' (p.71).

We end the exercise with a final round which begins, 'One thing I wish is…' This time, those agreeing with the sentiment must shake the speaker's hand.

I start. 'One thing I wish is that I was more confident.'

Grace, Allie, Jade, Pete and even Conor shake my hand. We say no more.

Pete says, 'One thing I wish is that I could meet Jordan!'

No one shakes his hand.

Ledley says, 'One thing I wish is that I'll always be able to talk to Karina's mum.'

No one shakes his hand because no one knows Karina's mum except Ledley.

Grace says, 'One thing I wish is that I could have talked to my mum before she died.'

'My mum's alive,' says Allie, 'but I wish I could have talked to my gran before she died.' She reaches across and shakes Grace's hand.

Again, we let this rest. We ask no questions.

Jade says, 'I wish people didn't get the wrong idea about me.'

We all shake her hand except Conor who obviously still hasn't forgiven her.

Allie says she wishes prejudice didn't exist and we all automatically shake her hand except for Conor.

It's his turn. 'I wish school wasn't such a pain in the arse.'

Jade and I are the only ones who don't shake his hand.

Then, as an afterthought, Jade says, 'Oh, go on, then!' and shakes his hand.

They're all looking at me.

'School's got its good points!' I say. 'It's not all bad!'

'Yeah, but you've got to say that though!' laughs Jade. 'You work here!'

I laugh as well. The exercise is finished.

'Can we do that teddy bear thing now?'

Poor Grace. I assure her that next week, for our final session, we'll start with something that'll be good fun.

'The teddy bear thing?'

'Maybe that, maybe something else.'

We do one more exercise. A member of the group sits with his back to the group. (Ledley immediately volunteers.) Silently, the rest of the group decides which member of the group they'll take turns to describe aloud but they're only allowed to describe *positive* things about that person. When we've all had a turn to say something, the person with his or her back to the group must guess who was being described.

Ledley turns his chair and sits with his back to the group. Gleefully, we point at each other before agreeing that we'll describe Pete.

Pete looks aghast. I explain that the person being described must obviously also say something positive. He looks even more aghast.

I begin. 'This person puts up with a lot but is still a really friendly person.'

Pete is curling with embarrassment.

Conor stumbles, 'This person's okay, I suppose.'

Allie says, 'This person can be a laugh sometimes.'

Jade says, 'This person's got a cool haircut.'

Delighted, Pete pretends to preen himself.

Grace says, 'This person's got dyslexia.'

I assume that this has given the game away but, surprisingly, Ledley doesn't react. I ask her to say what she thinks is *positive* about a person having dyslexia.

She doesn't know.

'Could be because this person tries to stay positive,' I suggest, 'or because this person is good at understanding other people with difficulties? Or because this person doesn't complain about something so frustrating?'

'But he does!'

'Okay, so what do you think is a *positive* thing about this person, Grace?'

'He lends me money!'

Pete himself goes last. He makes panicky, haven't-got-a-clue faces behind Ledley's back before saying, 'This person will do anything for a laugh.'

Ledley turns round. 'It's Pete!'

I congratulate Ledley on his triumph and we laugh because it was so easy.

Pete has a turn to be the guesser. We nominate Jade to be described and continue in this way with the nominated person obliged to hear positive things about themselves. And when the guesser sometimes gets it wrong, the wrongly guessed person is quietly pleased, remembering all the qualities that have just been mentioned.

As usual, interesting things get said. Pete describes Grace (with tits!) as 'good to talk to' and Conor, sensing how conciliatory she's been, admits that Jade is 'good at talking'.

About Conor himself, the object of their earlier derision, they are cautiously approving. Pete says he's 'a good laugh, when he wants to be'. Jade says he's 'very independent'. Grace says that Conor 'can say good things sometimes' and Allie describes him as 'someone who doesn't copy anyone'. Ledley, true to macho form, praises Conor for getting into trouble with the police.

Of course, there's plenty of projection in what they say – admiring qualities they'd like to be admired for themselves – but, however fleeting, these are important interactions: young people tentatively reaching out to one another within the framework of a safe enough group.

I remind them that next week will be our last.

FOURTH SESSION

Pete and Ledley are late. The rest of us are ready to begin but I'm reluctant to start explaining what we're doing if I'm going to have to explain it all over again for Pete and Ledley.

'Is this our last time?' asks Grace. 'Can't we go on longer?'

Jade sounds surprised. 'What? This is the last meeting? I thought you said it was six weeks?' She looks at me, imploringly. 'Go on! We're not missing anything important. The teachers won't mind if we miss more lessons!'

'Please!' begs Grace. 'It won't matter, honestly! This group's good!'

I re-affirm the fact that, sadly, we must end today.

'That's so stupid!' Jade says. 'We should be allowed to go on for longer if we want to. We all want to!'

Noisily, Pete and Ledley come in, both with stories about being kept behind by teachers for things which weren't their fault (being picked on!) and I wonder how much their lateness is an unconscious acknowledgement that, although I will almost certainly continue my individual meetings with each person, this truly is our last session as a group. It could be a complete coincidence; it could be that they really *were* kept behind by teachers, but some young people miss the last session of a group because saying goodbye to anyone is too unsettling. Perhaps lateness expresses a kind of ambivalence. Perhaps, through Pete and Ledley, the group is saying that we're sad this is ending because we'll miss it but, at the same time, we're not sad because this is difficult. If this is so then, somehow in this session, the group will have to find a way of acknowledging and tolerating these mixed feelings.

We start with the chairs pulled right back, creating a large space. The group is marooned on a desert island, sitting around a beautiful lagoon. They can swim safely in the beautiful lagoon (the floor) but there's one problem. From time to time, an enormous, hungry shark (me) will appear. However, the swimmers will be safe because the ever-vigilant lifeguard (me) will shout a warning whenever the shark appears. When the swimmers hear the shout, all they have to do is to get onto one of the rocks in the lagoon (large pieces of paper scattered on the floor) and stay on the rocks until the danger passes.

We begin with everyone walking around, pretending to be swimmers. After a minute, I scream 'Shark!' and they jump onto the various bits of paper, clinging to one another and laughing. The danger passes and they go back into the water. I apologise for not warning them before that the rocks have a tendency to get smaller (as I tear them in half) or disappear altogether.

The shark appears and, this time, manages to catch Allie before she can get onto a rock. I explain that, once you've been eaten by a shark, you *become* a shark. And off we go again.

These introductory exercises are more than 'games' and more than 'fun', although fun is very important. These exercises allow young people to *play* and, in my experience, young people don't play enough. Playing allows us to try out roles and practise situations. Through play, we learn (or don't learn) to collaborate, to confront, to excuse, to put up with short-term misfortune. These are all important ways in which a 'self' develops, stretches and becomes more adaptable.

This particular exercise also allows people to touch. Again, most young people are starved of touch – of touch that's appropriate and incidental, of touch that isn't self-conscious. Teenage boys, in particular, have usually avoided any physical contact with their mothers (too unmanly) and with their fathers and other boys (too homosexual) for *years*. Yet they're intensely physical – fighting, chasing, catching, wrestling. They sit in school sometimes, bristling with undischarged physical anxiety, and I've run groups with boys who can't think straight until some of this anxiety has been released. So they cling to each other, balancing on the imaginary rocks, given permission to touch by the circling shark. They love it.

'Get lost, Pete!'

'What's the matter?'

'Get lost! Move your chair away!'

The beautiful lagoon having vanished, we're now sitting in a re-convened circle and Pete's chair is evidently too close to Grace's.

He moves his chair. 'I wouldn't want to sit that close to you anyway,' he says. 'You're fat!'

'Like you're so gorgeous, Pete!' says Allie, sticking up for Grace.

Jade joins in. 'That's pathetic, saying stuff like that, Pete! You're such a wanker!'

Smirking, Pete looks at Ledley and Conor but gets no support. He's on his own and 'wanker' is an insult about being alone.

Jade turns to me. 'Aren't you going to tell him off?' she asks. 'That's really harsh, saying stuff like that. How would he like it if we said stuff about him?'

I'm caught between competing needs. On the one hand, I agree utterly with Jade – the last thing Grace needs is for comments to be made about her size. But on the other hand, I feel sorry for Pete because several things have crystallised. First, we've just done an exercise where people have been able to be physically close and Pete will have enjoyed that. Arguably, he was continuing something of that by leaving his chair so close to Grace's, although he was probably also sending a mixed message to Grace: I want to be closer to you *and* I want to annoy you by getting too close (and I don't know what to do with my ambivalence).

Second, this argument is really about *closeness*. There's been a degree of closeness in this group but now the group is ending. So, should the members of the group pursue that closeness or back away now, protecting themselves in anticipation of the ending?

Third, the argument is about sexuality which has been a recurring theme from the beginning of the group's life. It's interesting that Pete and Grace are the antagonists rather than

Ledley and Jade who, to some extent, have been the male and female leaders in the group. Perhaps, unconsciously, it's safer for the group to let Pete and Grace play these roles because a row between Ledley and Jade might risk the group's destruction. How on earth could a boy and a girl be 'close', they might wonder, without things becoming sexual?

And there's a fourth issue. The argument that's broken out is very childlike with Grace effectively complaining, 'I don't want to sit next to you!' and Pete bleating, 'Well, I don't want to sit next to you either!' Jade then asks the supervising parent (me) to sort out the squabble. It's characteristic of groups approaching an ending that members temporarily revert to childlike behaviour. *Because* they're ending, they feel afraid, de-skilled, dependent. The feeling passes but acknowledging it can be helpful. I'm not going to get caught up in arbitrating between the children and I'm not going to take their argument at face value. There are more important, unspoken issues being expressed.

'I was wondering how everyone feels about us ending,' I say, 'because people have shared lots of important things in this group and now it's ending. Sometimes, when something good comes to an end, we feel pretty weird about saying goodbye to the other people. In this group, I think we've tried to support each other and sometimes we've felt close to each other. I imagine some people might have things they want to say about that.'

'What d'you mean?' asks Allie. 'You mean, what have we liked about being in this group?'

'Not just that,' I say. 'What you've liked, what's been difficult, what's been frustrating, what you'll miss, how you're feeling about the other people in the group...'

Ledley says it's been good missing lessons.

Grace says she hasn't enjoyed having Pete in the group but that she's enjoyed the games. 'And we still haven't done that thing with the teddy bear!'

No one else says anything. I abandon my plan to do an exercise involving different chairs to represent our public and private selves because that would be too exposing. When a group is ending, most people need to gather up their defences rather than throw them away. Instead, we do a different exercise, providing a structure within which they'll be able talk to each other about how they feel.

I pull an extra chair into the circle, next to me on my immediate right. 'Whoever has the empty chair on their right can invite another member of the group to come and sit next to them for a reason,' I say. 'So, you might want someone to come and sit next to you because you like them or because they've been a good friend or because you've enjoyed getting to know them better or because you didn't like them but you feel differently about them now. It's up to you. The person being invited can decide whether that's a good enough reason, in which case they'll move, or, if it's not a good enough reason, they might want to know a bit more or they might want to ask you what you mean. When someone moves, there'll be an empty chair left behind and the person with *that* chair on their right will choose someone to invite. So, be thinking who you'll invite when the empty chair is next to you and what your reason will be.'

Conor immediately turns sideways on his chair – half in and half out of the group. The others are looking round at each other warily.

'I'll go first because the empty chair is on my right. Jade, I'd like you to come and sit next to me because I respect the way you stick up for yourself and other people.'

She beams and hurries across to the empty chair. Her old chair is now empty and on Conor's right.

He looks bemused. 'What do I have to do?'

'Think who you want to sit next to you and tell them why.'

'Can't think of anyone.'

'Keep thinking.'

'You, then.'

'Why?'

'Because you're all right.'

I move seats and my old chair is now on Ledley's right.

'Pete, sit next to me!'

Pete hesitates and asks, 'Hasn't he got to say why?'

I nod.

Ledley tuts. For him, this is dangerous – this intimacy, this saying things directly to people. He thinks. 'Because we support the same team!' Translated, this probably means, 'because you're a friend' and 'because I like you'.

Pete moves.

Shyly, Grace invites Allie to sit next to her. 'Because we weren't such good friends before but since we've been in this group together I've got to know you.'

I invite Ledley. 'Because I know you get into trouble for things but I like your sense of humour and I think you're a really nice guy when people get to know you and I wish more people had the chance to get to know you.'

He moves.

Jade pushes the group further. 'I'm inviting Conor because I know I've given you a hard time in this group, Conor, and I want to say I didn't mean it and you're all right really.'

Avoiding her eye, Conor shuffles across the circle.

Grace follows on. 'Conor, again, because you don't say a lot but you've joined in with everything and that's cool!'

Pete invites Ledley, 'Because you've stuck up for me in fights and I know I can count on you.'

Allie says she wants to invite the whole group but settles for Jade.

Pete invites Grace, 'To say sorry for what I said.'

Grace moves.

Conor invites Pete, 'Because I can't think of anyone else!'

Rightly, Pete stands his ground and doesn't move. 'That's not good enough!'

Conor winces. 'Because you're...sort of...like a mate.'

'That'll do!'

Eventually, I stipulate that we'll have another four moves and, after those, the exercise ends.

A lot has just happened. In a way, this exercise has been the culmination of our time together, allowing members of the group to say things to each other that they wouldn't normally dream of saying. These things are possible to say because of the tantalising structure of the exercise (will I be asked and who will I ask?) but – more importantly – because of the culture which has developed in the group. During our time together, each person has been 'recognised'. Defences have been respected, not stripped away. Once a vulnerable 'self' feels understood and feels understandable, it becomes possible to acknowledge other people, play with other people, recognise *other* people. Relationships become possible.

For fun, we do an exercise which gets everyone groaning, pleading, shrieking with laughter as they accumulate more and more lipstick smudges on their faces.

Four minutes left. We go round the group, one last time. Each person has to say two things that have been good about the group and one thing that's been difficult.

Jade offers to start. 'It's been good that we've all got on and it's been good finding out about people. A difficult thing was when people didn't want to talk.'

We continue round the circle.

'Good thing was the teddy bear thing,' says Grace, 'which we *still* haven't done like you said we would! Another good thing was getting to know Allie better. Well, getting to know everybody, really. And a difficult thing was worrying about what other people would think.'

There's a stillness in the room.

'This group has been really good,' Pete says, 'because I feel like I can get on with everyone now. Even Grace!' he laughs. 'And I hope we'll always get on. And I liked that sharks thing.'

I push him to think of something difficult.

'What I said to Grace,' he says. 'Sorry, Grace.'

'It's okay.' She smiles at him.

Ledley says, 'A good thing was missing the lessons. Another good thing was that we didn't fight. And it was bad when we had arguments.'

We're acknowledging that we have mixed feelings about this group as about most things. I say it's been interesting learning about being different and being the same. I say I've enjoyed being in the group and found it difficult when I haven't known what to say next.

Allie says that the group has surprised her and she's sorry that it's ending.

Bearing in mind the losses which have hurt her in the past, I ask Allie what she'll remember, what she'll keep from the experience of being in the group.

'I'll remember that people listened to each other and I'll remember Conor.'

'Because?'

'Because it must have been hard for him in this group.'

'What about a difficult thing?'

'Feeling embarrassed, doing some of the games.'

Everyone looks at Conor, the last person to speak.

He shrugs. 'I agree with you lot. It's been pretty good. It's been good not getting hassled and when people have said things.'

'Something difficult?'

'Dunno, really. Me?'

NOTES

1. Axline (1966) famously describes this process in her work with a very withdrawn six-year-old boy.

2. Interestingly, Plummer (2007) defines 'self-esteem' as the difference between a person's perceived sense of themselves (Pete's 'I'm crap!', perhaps) and their ideal self (perhaps Allie's 'I want to be like Gemma!').

3. Projective identification (Klein 1946) is the unconscious process whereby a person defends themselves against a feeling by getting someone *else* to feel it. And because the feeling resonates with that other person, he or she *does* feel it and starts behaving accordingly.

CHAPTER 3

A Fragmented Self

With the English words he knows, Bashkim describes running from the gunfire into the hills above his village – running so fast, he says, that his feet hit the backs of his legs. I ask what happened next.

'I lost myself.'

He means that he got lost in the hills and he goes on to tell me about meeting other refugees, also escaping, who looked after him because his parents and his sister were missing. But his erratic English tells another truth because, in a sense, he did lose his self. His parents and sister have still not been found. They may have gone to another refugee camp or they may have been killed. They may be alive somewhere or dead somewhere – he has no idea. A fifteen-year-old boy, transported by kindly people away from the war to the safety of another country and now meeting with a strange man called a counsellor, it's as if Bashkim really has lost his original self.

It's sometimes argued that psychotherapeutic work with young asylum seekers like Bashkim is impossible. These people are too fragile, it is said. Their practical needs are too urgent. They can't sustain a relationship for long enough to absorb the benefits.

There's some truth in these claims. Therapeutic work with young asylum seekers is certainly different from work with people who have lived in one country all their life and have never experienced war, torture, imprisonment, rape or the killing of their family. Asylum seekers *are* fragile and their practical needs *are* urgent. But so is their need to connect with other human beings who (regardless of whether or not they are counsellors) can be reliable, kind and tenacious. Therapeutic relationships are not only possible but crucial. The therapeutic task might be described as making meaning out of meaninglessness, as learning to live with despair or as learning to attach again to strangers in an unfair world. In this chapter I want to describe a further sense in which therapeutic work with young asylum seekers like Bashkim is also about putting back together a self which has become fragmented.

From the very beginning of our lives we're preoccupied with putting ourselves together, with locating and learning to control an arm, a leg, a mouth. We develop a series of gestures and responses and learn to co-ordinate all these things in order to communicate and survive. But we have the potential to lose that control and to fragment at any time in our lives. Wolf (1988) defines fragmentation as 'regression of the self toward lessened cohesion, more permeable boundaries, diminished energy and vitality, and disturbed and disharmonious balance' (p.39). Characteristic of what used to be called a nervous breakdown is losing that physical control, losing that cohesion and becoming dependent on other people again. The self breaks down.

Kohut (1971) argues that we all have a deeply rooted, unconscious fear of fragmentation: the fear that our self, protected by carefully built up and controlled defences, will one day break down. All will be lost. We'll no longer be able to think or function in the world. We'll become fragmented into so many psychological pieces that we won't know who we are. Perhaps because of this unconscious fear, Stern (1985) describes our 'central tendency', even as infants, 'to order the world by seeking invariants' (p.74). In other words, we deal with the threat of fragmentation, we hold ourselves together by finding and clinging to things that won't change. For babies, the most important invariant is a mother or mothering-figure. With luck, she can be internalised at an early age so that, even when she's not physically there, we can hold onto her memory and hold our selves together.

Young asylum seekers are no different from other young people *except* that they've experienced far more extreme situations and these situations have affected them far more dramatically. All young people are preoccupied with issues of loss and adaptation but most have grown up in environments which haven't changed very much, which have contained them, kept them safe and allowed them to experiment, trying out different parts of themselves, developing a repertoire of roles they can play to meet all occasions. Because this maternal, mirroring environment was safe enough, these roles, these selves have expanded but still cohere. The young person has developed a clear and flexible sense of *who I am* and *how I can be.*

Asylum seekers have been through experiences where there were no invariants, where *everything* changed. As a result, they struggle to make sense of what's happened and put together an identity, a self which will keep fragmentation at bay until they're confident enough to re-enter the world. For them, there's no longer a containing, safe environment within which to grow. However resilient a person may be (and asylum seekers can be *very* resilient), traumatic experience potentially breaks down a young person's sense of identity into disparate parts, no longer cohering. Some asylum seekers will have been lucky enough as infants to develop a secure sense of self in the arms and gaze of a loving mother. But subsequent events will have broken that self down into dislocated, anxious selves.

The idea of a self consisting of many 'selves' is similar to Moreno's (1946) idea that a self is made up of a cluster or repertoire of *roles,* some of them particular to the individual and learned from birth (I'm a hungry self, an angry self, a cold self), some of them learned in response to and on behalf of other people (I'm a funny self, a smiling self, an obedient self). Moreno's notion is that experience limits or expands the roles we're able to play. He suggests that we're happiest and most truly 'ourselves' when we can spontaneously play all sorts of roles in response to all sorts of situations. In that sense, asylum seekers are very limited. They're obliged and able to play only certain roles because of the uncertainty and cruelty of their situations.

I want to describe what I mean by these roles, these 'selves'.

A DEVELOPMENTAL SELF

Angelin arrived in the UK only days after the murder of his parents. He was fifteen. I started seeing him five months later, by which time he'd got used to living in a strange country. He'd begun to learn English, although we met with an interpreter for the time being.

For many young asylum seekers, the normal developmental processes of growing up are interrupted by the events which precipitated their flight to another country. Families are scattered, parents are lost: all the certainties of life are taken away. Normal adolescent developmental processes – physical, emotional, psychological, sexual – are even harder to negotiate when the whole world has changed.

Angelin had never had brothers or sisters and now he had no parents. If he'd once been a boy separating gradually from his parents, becoming slowly more independent, practising relationships with peers at school during the day before returning to the safety of his home at night, that process was now stopped. He was suddenly an adult – dealing with solicitors, immigration officials, money, food. He was washing his own clothes, getting himself up in the mornings for school, deciding what to do in the evenings. His social worker visited him and his teachers talked to him at school but, effectively, he was on his own.

He talked easily about life leading up to the death of his parents. He talked about hearing gunshots, running away and coming back later to find his parents' bodies in the house, killed because of their ethnic origin. He didn't cry. When we talked about the future, he said he wanted to study hard, go to university and become a manager.

I suggested that he was already a 'manager'. He looked unimpressed.

He seemed to like talking with me and the interpreter, however, and, as the weeks went by, his English got better and better. Now we spoke mostly in English with the interpreter intervening only when she sensed he was stuck or needed to stay in his home language in order to go with the flow of whatever he was saying.

So, after a while, I suggested that we might no longer need our interpreter. This would give Angelin more independence, I reasoned. Her job was done.

Angelin said no. He liked having her there, he said, even though he didn't need her as much as he once had.

I demurred before realising what this might mean. With her there, we were a reconstituted family – father, mother and son. Of course he needed her less obviously than before because he was fifteen years old, not five. Of course he spoke mostly to me because he was a macho boy, keen to establish himself with men. Of course she appeared to be no longer necessary. But she was. She was needed in the same way that all teenage boys pretend not to need their embarrassing, controlling mothers any more while secretly needing these mothers to stay just as they are. I think that what Angelin valued about our meetings had less to do with the content of our conversations and more to do with the experience of being with a man and woman who felt warmly towards him, were pleased to see him, were interested in what he had to say and were approving of his daily achievements. If the death of his real parents had propelled Angelin into premature adulthood, he was now going back in time and resuming the process of separating more gradually from two pretend parents – telling us grandiose stories with snippets of how he really felt, telling us about his life now with snippets from the past – slowly reconnecting the emerging adult and lingering child.

A CULTURAL SELF

Toni is cooler than a cucumber, brighter than a button. In fact, he's more English than the English boys he hangs out with – his street accent perfected, his clothes exactly chosen to fit the current fashion. He's a wide boy, a rude boy, a gangsta boy. And he's also a fourteen-year-old asylum-seeking boy who, with his father, escaped ethnic cleansing. He's a boy who doesn't know whether his mother is alive or dead.

He's ambivalent about meeting with me. Sometimes he comes late and sometimes he doesn't come at all. He's disinclined to talk about himself, preferring to ask me about how my week has been, about my family and what I do in my spare time. I think there's a part of him that wants to invest in our relationship because he knows that I like him and enjoy his company. But he also knows that I know there's more to him than the gum-chewing, grinning, charming exterior. He knows I know that it's not that simple.

Some asylum seekers and refugees try to do what Toni has done so successfully: they try to become assimilated into their new culture to such an extent that no one will know the difference and they can convince themselves that there never was another life. But the old life always catches up with them – in dreadful nightmares, on the television news and because they can only deceive themselves intermittently.

I draw an outline of two Tonis, one on the left and one on the right-hand side of the page. I label them Past Toni and Present Toni. I explain to him that some people in his position try to tear the page in half, screwing up the Past and throwing it into the bin. I fold the page in half with Past Toni now folded behind Present Toni. I say that this is how it is for most of us – our past selves are hidden behind our present selves. I say that the two halves have to learn to be friends and I open the paper out again to illustrate a more open relationship between the two selves.

He seems to understand. But he's nervous. It's painful to recall the past and from time to time there's racist bullying in his school so it pays to be like everyone else. Toni's chosen to hide in the long grass of Englishness and, in effect, I'm waiting in a clearing, calling out to him, promising that the bad people have gone away and that it's safe to come out now.

From time to time, he does come out – telling me incidental stories about the past, taking some of the opportunities I offer to link the past and present as we talk about the weather in this country compared to his old country, the differences in food and in schools, the ways in which girls are similar and different, the ways parents treat their children in different countries.

I continue to enjoy his Englishness – the highlights in his hair, his designer trainers, his knowledge of pop music. If I dismantled this façade, he wouldn't come back – and rightly so – because he would have been unfairly exposed. To some extent, he *does* have to assimilate this new culture. He has to get by. He has to fit in. My task is to help him recognise the old and new parts of himself *simultaneously* so that he no longer has to be so painfully split.

The split *is* painful. Another young person I'm working with, Raman, has a cut on his forehead and some swelling around one eye. I ask if he's been in a fight. Through our interpreter, he says no, he fell over. I doubt whether this is true, so I ask more and he says that he hit his head on the toilet. I ask what happened and, embarrassed, he admits he'd been drinking.

I happen to know that Raman hasn't been going to school. That was one of the reasons why his social worker suggested he might like to talk with a counsellor. That, and the fact that he's a sixteen-year-old boy whose parents and siblings were killed, who speaks little English and knows almost no one in the country where he has now arrived, seeking asylum. I also know that, in his home country, education is the most important prize for a good child. In his home country, drunkenness is for failures, for people shaming their families.

When he talks about his mother, he begins to cry. He takes tissues and presses them into his eyes. He can't speak.

I wait until his sobbing subsides. I say something bland about his mother being proud of him for surviving so well.

He shakes his head vigorously. 'I have betrayed my mother,' he says through the interpreter. 'I have betrayed her!' He cries again.

I begin to realise the significance of getting drunk and not going to school. They express something of his loneliness and despair. But they exacerbate the situation because then he feels that he's not living up to his parents' expectations, not making up for their deaths and not honouring their memory like a good son. He's betraying his family, betraying his culture.

We talk more about his dead mother – about what she looked like, the things she said and did, all the memories he has of her. I promise to write something about her in his name as a keepsake for him. I suggest this because Raman's sense is that he's lost her, lost everything about her. He can't speak to her in his head because she's dead, he says, *dead*.

The next time we meet, I present him with what I've written. He reads it through and is clearly moved. I ask what he would like to change and he says there's nothing. He folds the paper away carefully and puts it in his bag.

Raman is re-connecting less punitively with his past. By giving him back the mother who loved him, we can now talk more easily about his old and new lives. The past is gone but is no longer 'dead'. We can be sad about it, we can mourn it but we can also take from it all that's precious and useful. On Raman's behalf, I've included in the piece, 'My mother loved me. She was kind. When I was growing up and I did things that were wrong, she always forgave me.'

He hasn't contradicted this. For him, drinking and not going to school were ways of cutting off from the past. They were ways of trying to be a different person. My hope is that – however painful it may be – he can embrace the past and connect it again to the present.

A STUDENT SELF

In many cultures, people are defined by their jobs. Whether their job is as a doctor, mechanic, shepherd, soldier or teacher, it brings clear social status and some sense of what the future might hold. Adult asylum seekers lose that sense of a professional self when they're not allowed to work.

Young asylum seekers are allowed to go to school, however, and school offers many things which are attractive, whether a person is already well-educated or has no formal education at all. School fills the day. School is an opportunity to make friends, to be with caring adults. As in Raman's case, school represents the hopes and expectations of a family. In the event of being deported, education is something useful to take away from a country where you're no longer welcome. So, potentially, school represents a very important part of one's self. But a self which can be snatched away at any time.

Kameel has always told me how much he likes school. We've always made our counselling appointments for later in the day so that he never misses out on anything at school. Now he announces angrily that he doesn't want to go any more. 'There is no point!'

It turns out that his asylum case will be heard in court next month and his solicitor has warned him that it's unlikely to be successful.

'I will not go school. They put me on a plane to my country and I be killed!'

I don't know what to say.

'I tell my teacher I am leaving!'

I ask what she said about that. He tuts and says nothing, from which I deduce that he probably *hasn't* spoken to his teacher but this is what he *feels* like saying to her. I say I'm not surprised that he feels like giving up after all his hard work.

His anger melts a little and he looks sad. 'I try hard,' he says, tearfully. 'Every day I work to learn good English. I am good student!'

'I know you are,' I say. 'I know.'

'I go school every day. When I sick. When I cold. Every day I go school.'

We talk together about the agony of not knowing. Because every day young asylum seekers like Kameel go to school and have to strike a balance between the promise of school, the hope of a stable future, and the uncertainty of whether or not they'll be allowed to stay in this country. Will all that education be useful or will it all have been a cruel waste of time?

On a cool September evening, I see another young asylum seeker, Ylli, in the street. We met regularly when he first arrived in this country, talking about the awfulness he'd left behind and his hopes for the future. He was studying hard and enjoying A levels. 'For me, physics is like playing!' I remember him saying with a smile.

He tells me that he got top grades in maths, further maths and physics. I congratulate him and ask what he's doing now, aware that the government doesn't fund asylum seekers to go on to university.

'I'm working a few hours a week in the newspaper shop by the train station,' he says.

I ask what that's like.

'It's okay,' he says, ruefully. 'I see people from my class. They did not get such good grades. They come to the shop to buy a paper from me. They are going on the train. They are going to university.'

A SOCIAL SELF

Abdul expects to get his own way. When doctors can't cure him, when social workers can't provide answers, when solicitors can't make promises, he sulks, he strops, he stomps off swearing.

He does this with me, too. I can't cure his bad back, I can't get him a house with his friends, I can't get him permission to stay in this country. I can't do anything very much except listen and talk. So I'm pretty useless. And from time to time with Abdul I *do* feel useless, although I'm experienced enough to know that this is almost certainly his feeling, projected into me.

He tries everything – coming late, leaving early, refusing to talk, wanting his friend to be our interpreter, wanting me to do him practical favours. I withstand the barrage. I have no choice because until we've got past this behaviour there will be no trust between us. I *must* withstand his bullying or I'll be just another person he can manipulate and never trust.

Over several torrid months, we meet, we talk and I manage to hold my ground despite his scorn and the pressure he puts on me to dislike him and end our meetings. 'He's just a boy,' I keep telling myself. 'He's upset and sad and this is the only way he knows of dealing with the situation. *Keep* liking him. *Stay* patient. Try to enjoy being with him. Remember that he's choosing to come every week.'

Things begin to change. He stops asking for favours. He starts coming on time. And he begins to tell me more about his life before the terrible events which brought him to this country. Everybody was scared of his father whose powerful position in the secret police meant that Abdul and his brothers were feared locally. If Abdul wanted something, then someone would get it for him because they were scared. They were also resentful, he admits one day. He had lots of power but no friends. When he played football, the other boys would always let him win and let him be the goalscorer.

I'm about to laugh at the pointlessness of a football game like this until I realise how important the story is. Abdul is telling me what he needs from me. In our football matches, he needs me *not* to surrender. He needs me *not* to be scared. He needs me *not* to be taken in by the tough, stroppy exterior, his false self (Winnicott 1965), but to be aware of another self hidden away, a self feeling useless, friendless, stuck. In effect, he needs me to be a proper friend.

From this moment our relationship begins to change. But slowly. He's obviously never had a 'friend' like this before. It's a new experience and he doesn't always know how to interpret my warmth or friendliness. It takes him a long time to realise that I'm not going to use what I know in order to manipulate him.

Abdul is one of many asylum seekers who develop a false self (usually a tough, I-don't-care self but sometimes a crumbling, I-can't-cope self) as a way of dealing with other people. To some extent, we all have a false self which helps us to deal with things. The problem is when that false self becomes stuck – when the wind changes and that self becomes all that other people know of us. The problem is acute for asylum seekers who must leave one culture for another culture where the rules are different, where the social hierarchy is different and, in Abdul's case, where bullying behaviour no longer works. They must learn new ways of being with other people.

A LOVEABLE SELF

Amaka's eyes fill with tears whenever we mention the subject because her life turns on the answer. When she was twelve, living with her mother and sister in a refugee camp, she woke up one morning and her mother was gone.

We've discussed this many times – whether her mother left because she didn't love her children, whether she couldn't care for them any more, whether she was forced to abandon them by unscrupulous men or whether, Amaka wonders, her mother was eaten by a lion.

'Why did she go?' she asks, gazing ahead. She's trying her best, studying hard at college. She goes to church. She puts up with the sapping uncertainty of being an asylum seeker. Her question is really about whether or not she was loved by her mother because the answer to that question puts her whole life into perspective.

I say that it's hard for a mother to leave her children. I tell her about the film *Sophie's Choice*, where a mother is forced to choose between her two children.

Still Amaka gazes blankly ahead. She finds it hard to meet with me regularly, partly because she knows that from time to time we'll discuss her mother, and partly because she finds it hard to attach to someone who might become a parent-figure. If she allows herself to meet with me regularly, she might start looking forward to meetings, she might start relying on them and then where would she be? She could be abandoned at any time. So 'Why did she go?' has become her central question.

She tells me absently about the nursery where she's helping as part of her childcare course and about how, yesterday, when it was time to finish, one mother didn't arrive to collect her child. 'Why did she do that?' asks Amaka.

My job isn't to convince Amaka that she *was* loved by her mother and is therefore loveable now. It's certainly possible that she was loved – she has good memories of her mother and I encourage her to share and enjoy these memories with me. My job is to help her bear the sense of *not knowing* and offer her, in the meantime, an experience of mattering to an adult who respects her privacy, isn't scared of her sadness, remembers the smallest details of her life, listens very carefully to what she says and is obviously always pleased to see her. Amaka will draw her own conclusions.

There are plenty of other Amakas. There are young asylum seekers who have sometimes been forced to do bad things in order to survive and who are left feeling unloveable. There are young people whose original, formative experience of being loved was fleeting, ambiguous, compromised or simply non-existent. The danger for all of them is that they look for external proof of their worth (money, clothes, sexiness) to compensate for the lack of an internal sense of being loveable that they can believe in and trust.

A FILIAL SELF

Psychotherapy involves making sense of our parents. Or making a different kind of sense. Like any young people, there are asylum seekers who have never met one or sometimes both of their parents, who grew up with a violent, alcoholic or depressed parent, with parents who separated or with parents who had affairs. Asylum seekers carry these legacies like anyone else. But they also carry the additional legacy of their parents' disappearance or death, of their parents' complicity sometimes in brutal crimes or of their parents' powerlessness in the face of massacre, torture, persecution.

Our parents are not meant to disappear or be killed. They're not meant to be cruel and they're not meant to be powerless when we need them to protect us. Making sense of *these* parents is particularly hard. Because of his political involvement, Subira's father left on her thirteenth birthday without telling her. Muhammad's parents were killed at night when he was far away, sleeping in a field, guarding the sheep. Nia's father regularly beat and may have killed her mother. Brehan's father was in charge of a prison where political prisoners were held and, when the government was overthrown, Brehan's father disappeared.

Brehan is a loyal son. He says that his father always looked after the family. They had a nice house and a nice car. He and his father played football together sometimes when his father wasn't at work. But his father was at work a lot, Brehan says.

I can leave his story unchallenged. It's not my job to spoil good memories and I'm sure Brehan's father was wonderful in all sorts of ways. The problem is that the story Brehan is telling himself (or, at least, telling me) is so simple. Some young people hold on to a simplified story of their life because a more complex truth is too much to bear. When so much is changing, some things have to stay the same. At least for now. The problem comes in the future when Brehan starts to think about the desultoriness of his life and the fact that his father shows no sign of rescuing him from it. He knows that his father is probably dead. He also knows that his life *now* is directly linked to his father's work *then*. Were it not for his father, the family wouldn't have enjoyed such a privileged lifestyle. Were it not for his father, he wouldn't now be living in a damp room in a shared house in a country where people make racist remarks in the street and a gang of boys from another country want to beat him up.

It's time for a re-think.

'My father was always worried about our safety.'

'Because of his job?'

'Yes. We had to go to school every day in a special car.'

'What was that like?'

'It was normal,' Brehan says. 'I didn't think about it.'

'Because you were young?'

He nods.

'And now?' I ask. 'What do you think about it now?'

'I wish it was different.'

I say nothing. Brehan is re-thinking.

He goes on, 'I wish my father had another job.'

I keep quiet.

'I might be living in my country with my family.'

This is the beginning of a much longer dialogue Brehan will have with himself – weighing up the father who provided so much against the father who risked so much – making sense, making a new story about a father who was wonderful in many ways and (probably) flawed in others; making sense of a son who wants to be loyal but finds that uncritical loyalty is becoming impossible.

A GENDERED SELF

> I'm a man but I cry like a woman. I'm a man and I must avenge my family but I feel scared like a woman. I'm a man and I must be full of life but I feel depressed like a woman. I'm a man. I will never find a woman.

For an asylum seeker, it's hard to know what's expected any longer of oneself as a young man or woman. The world has changed. The rules are different.

> I'm a woman but I must become like a man to survive. I'm a woman but I feel angry and violent like a man. I'm a woman and I must dress well but, if I do that, men will come after me. I'm a woman. Without my family, I will never find a man.

I talk with boys about feeling powerless and with girls about using their power. It's hard for boys and girls who've grown up in sexist societies where expectations are sometimes very fixed to know how to behave in a new environment where everything seems suddenly to be turned upside down. My own Western, liberal assumption is that it's good for boys to experience powerlessness once in a while and good for girls to experience being powerful because it goes against the stereotype. But my assumption is my own and simplistic. It's really hard to bear the feeling of powerlessness if you've always been used to power and it's really hard to find the confidence to take power when you've never had any in your life.

I listen to tears and indignation, rage and apprehension – young men and women learning new ways.

A SOMATIC SELF

Around her head Gukunda has wound a scarf – yellow, green and purple. Last week her head was uncovered with her hair braided elaborately and beautifully. The week before that, her hair was flat but decorated with coloured ribbons, woven intricately. Each week I remark that her latest creation looks wonderful. And each week she tells me how much her head hurts, as if it's splitting, she says, as if the skin is on fire, as if she has a knife in her brain.

She's been to the doctor who can find nothing wrong. She can't remember being beaten around the head during her time in prison although she does have appalling memories of blood in the streets and of hearing people being killed while she was hiding. She can't sleep. She asks for help with her head.

I explain that I'm not a doctor but that, as a counsellor, I know that bad memories are sometimes expressed through our bodies. I say that her head is hurting because she's seen and remembers so much.

She asks what can be done to help with this and I say that, sometimes, learning to talk about the things she remembers can help the memories to lose their power and can help the body to heal. She looks bemused. I say that, if we keep meeting and keep talking, her head will slowly get better.

She smiles obediently.

I believe this. I believe that our bodies remember *physically* the things we've experienced. Gukunda's problem is that it hurts to talk and it hurts not to talk. And it's very frightening when her head can't keep out the bad thoughts. It feels as if a barrier has been broken, as if her body is no longer under her control.

Agim is similar. He describes a tightening pain in his chest and around his heart; he describes breathlessness, palpitations, dizziness and a constant ache in his head. Again, the doctors have found nothing.

When he was eleven, Agim came home to find his village ablaze. Tanks had rumbled in and opened fire on all the houses. He felt numb, he says. There was no one around so he went into the hills where, for two years, he lived in forests with people he met, freezing cold for much of the time. 'My body was cold always,' he tells me, motioning from his neck downwards.

I suggest to him that his heart may still be frozen.

He looks at me as if I'm slightly mad. He thinks I mean that his heart is frozen – literally. I try to explain the metaphor. I ask how he felt when he saw his village burning.

He shrugs.

I persist.

Still he can't say anything. It dawns on me that he has no vocabulary for feelings and so the next time we meet I have with me a long list of 'feeling' words (sad, angry, afraid, abandoned) with their exact translation into Agim's language. From now on, whenever I ask how he feels or how he felt (and I deliberately ask a lot), we refer to the list and try to identify a word or two which best describes the feeling. I tell him that we are unfreezing his heart.

He eyes me with mild amusement, humouring this strange idea. But the idea is a true one. Agim's body is speaking his feelings because his mouth can't speak them. By equipping him with words, we'll begin to take some of the pressure off his body.

A SEXUAL SELF

I'm asking Habib about his love life – not teasing him but giving him an opportunity to talk because the young asylum seekers I know rarely, if ever, mention sex and yet sex, I sense, is a preoccupation, a constant source of anxiety, anger, shame and frustration. I ask whether he ever goes out with girls.

He shakes his head. 'Girls say what have you got and I say I have nothing,' he says, clearly missing any innuendo. I think he means that girls ask him if he has money, a car or a job and he says he has none of these things. 'Who am I,' he asks, 'when I have nothing?'

It's hard to talk about sex. It's hard to find words which bring together the physical and the emotional. It's easier to keep the two separate. The idea of 'longing', for example, gets separated into either 'lusting' or 'missing'. People usually make this split as they talk about the physicality of sex or the emotionality of love. Not both. Not together.

I sense that both matter for Habib. He's terribly lonely and his loneliness is both physical and emotional. It's not my intention to pry but, rather, to let him talk in order to lessen his shame. In many cultures, masturbation is shameful, a sign of weakness, sinfulness. All-seeing gods are especially scornful. And masturbatory fantasies are complex because some asylum seekers have been raped, sometimes repeatedly; some have been forced into other sexual acts; some have viewed especially bizarre pornography. It's much easier, under these circumstances, to separate the physical and the emotional, to reduce sex to a perfunctory, physical spasm and keep love as something quite different. It's sometimes necessary to do this in order to survive. In rape, for example, it may have been necessary to keep body and feelings separate in order to survive.

Habib is saying nothing.

I say that it's difficult being a young man with no wife.

He nods.

I say it's difficult when we want to be close to someone but there's no one there.

Again he nods.

I say it's difficult when we see a beautiful woman in the street and hear other men boasting about having lots of sex.

Still he says nothing. (It crosses my mind that he may actually know very little about conventional sex and that I might need to do some explaining at some point in the future.) But he's listening and I go on, naming what I imagine may be some of his frustrations, desires, embarrassments, unspoken thoughts, but couching them in a generalised language about 'men' and 'us' and things being *generally* difficult or frustrating or unfair.

My hope is that by naming these things but attributing them to men generally, Habib's isolation and shame are lessened so that he's no longer the *only* man feeling what he's feeling. In fact, he's normal.

A SPIRITUAL SELF

Kamau has just learned from his solicitor that his appeal to stay in the UK has failed. He'll be deported whenever the officials get round to it. He tells me this and begins to cry, sliding from his chair onto the floor in front of me where he lies, curled up and sobbing. His mother told him that education was the future and that if he was good, if he studied hard, he would be rewarded. She told him that God was good and God would always protect him.

I sit on the floor with him, trying to keep thinking, trying to know what best to say and how to say it. His sobs cut through me. I say that he *is* good; he *has* done his best.

He wails.

I say that what's happened *isn't* fair. It's *not* what he deserves.

I'm not sure if he understands or even hears. But my job is to sit with him and be able to do nothing. That, I know, is something. When we fall to pieces (and Kamau's sliding to the floor is a kind of falling to pieces) the least that another person can do is simply to stay with us without getting scared, without running off into intellectual manoeuvres or defensive, practical suggestions. Practical suggestions can come later.

Western therapeutic models tend to assume that people are ultimately alone in the world, that they have choice about what they do with their lives and that their capacity to make relationships is what sustains them. This may all be true. But many asylum seekers feel sustained by a faith in God or Allah, Jesus or the Prophet Mohammed. In that relationship they are never abandoned. In that relationship they will always be with other people in a church or in a mosque. And in that relationship there are models of suffering which compare with their own. We talk about Jesus's anger at the money-lenders, his despair on the cross. We talk about what it must have been like for the Prophet Mohammed not to be believed. Asylum seekers know all about anger and despair. They know what it's like not to be believed. We talk also about not knowing why bad things happen. We speculate. We wonder. We acknowledge that not knowing is normal.

I'm older. I have grey hair. I'm repeatedly asked by young asylum seekers, 'Why did this happen to me? What did I do to deserve this? Will life ever be different?'

They wait for an answer.

I say I don't know.

They look disappointed. But I hope they feel relieved.

Wiping his tears, Kamau asks, 'Why?'

I'm reduced to silence. Nothing I can say will help and I won't patronise him with platitudes. 'Why?' is a good question.

He gets back onto his chair.

I ask about his mother, about her life and how she coped with her own suffering. I ask what she would say to him now, attempting to find the inner voice which must have sustained Kamau through the terrible things that happened before he came to this country.

But he's too upset to think clearly. I'm jumping ahead, perhaps trying to give him something to take away because our meeting is about to end. Perhaps I'm asking about this for my own benefit.

He says nothing. When it's time to finish, he gets up, shakes my hand, thanks me politely and goes out, head down, thinking his own thoughts.

I'm left with the feeling of uselessness.

Kamau's story doesn't end happily. Reluctantly, he comes to see me a few more times and then stops. Every so often I ring to say that I'm thinking about him and that it will be good to see him again. But he never comes back. I'm left with my own sense of futility, my own sense of not being good enough. My theorising tells me that these are Kamau's feelings, projected and left with me because they're too much for him. But in my heart I know that they're also my feelings, my own sense of the limits of human kindness.

FRAGMENTED SELVES

Like Kamau, Habib, Gukunda, Agim, Brehan, Amaka, Abdul, Ylli, Kameel, Raman, Toni and Angelin, we're all made up of socially constructed selves. For a young asylum seeker, arriving alone in a strange country and speaking little or no English, *who I am* is no longer straightforward. It's hard to think about your self (your selves) when the priority is to exist, to act, to survive. It's hard to think about an internal world when you're still defined so powerfully by the external world, forced to react to other people and events, able to make few personal choices. The

danger is that the selves stay fragmented. And this may be necessary as a way of surviving a changed world where it's safer to
simplify or reduce oneself to something less vulnerable.

Regardless of what's happened in their lives, there are young
asylum seekers who were deprived of emotional warmth and
parental responsiveness from birth and so developed little sense
of a self from the beginning. Without that initial mirroring,
parental relationship, it's hard for anyone to make sense of what
they feel. A standard how-are-you-feeling question is often met
with incomprehension.

'My shoulder is hurting me.'

'Yes, but how are you feeling *inside?*'

'I don't know.'

Who I am is a limited concept. *I'm an asylum seeker. I go to
school. I watch television. I eat food. I go to sleep at night (if I'm lucky). I
don't know how I feel inside. I can't tell you that.*

There are asylum seekers whose traumatic experiences have,
in effect, stopped them thinking clearly (Rothschild 2000)
because, escaping from the danger they faced, instinct took over.
In neurological terms, the cerebral cortex (the thinking part of
the brain) stopped working properly because the amygdala (the
primitive fear response in the brain) overwhelmed the
hippocampus (the part which helps the cerebral cortex make
sense of what's happening). It can take a long time for this
neurological effect to correct itself.

But talking helps. Like all counselling, work with young
asylum seekers is dependent on the quality of a relationship
between two human beings. One human being (the counsellor)
acts as a mirror, helping the other to see and make sense of him
or her self. To begin with, that mirror, that self appears cracked,
fragmented – smashed even. So for therapists and other
professionals supporting asylum seekers there are important
hours to be spent simply listening to a person's story –
remembering it, piecing it together, thinking about it, putting it

in chronological order, exploring its different parts. Without an autobiography, we don't exist. We mean nothing. Therapy with young asylum seekers – whether it takes the form of meeting and talking regularly with a counsellor in the ways I've described or enjoying equally productive and important relationships with teachers, social workers and friends – is about starting to think again, to tell a story, to make sense of *who I am*, putting the half-formed, fragmented selves back together, alongside one another, overlapping with one another, interconnected with one another.

CHAPTER 4

A 'School' Self

> I hate school! It's such a load of crap. The teachers don't care.
> The lessons are totally pointless. Nobody's bothered. We
> just muck about all the time and get into trouble!

Some young people insist that school means absolutely nothing
to them and yet spend an awfully long time insisting on this,
taking the opportunity to disparage everything about their
school – the terrible teachers, the outrageous incidents – and
rejoicing in their many gleeful triumphs over the system. They
usually protest too much to be convincing. Even in the brief
blast of invective above, key adolescent issues abound – hatred,
care, pointlessness, play, rule-breaking. Clearly, school matters.
But can a young person really be said to have a 'relationship'
with a school? And, if so, how exactly does that relationship
affect a young person's development, a young person's
'self-esteem'?

Winnicott (1964) famously jokes that 'there is no such thing
as a baby' (p.88) because, at the very beginning of its life, a
baby's identity is inseparable from its mother's. I've often
wondered whether there's really no such thing as a school
because our sense of 'school' is always such an expression of
ourselves. Politicians find themselves talking about 'school' and
'schools' whenever they're worried about social cohesion or

disintegration, moral rectitude or decline, cultural diversity or the failure of law and order. Similarly, five ordinary people talking about a particular school can sound as if they're talking about five different schools because the idea of 'school' is so personal, evoking for each person an experience of childhood, of parenting, of hope and disappointment, of all that they've come to believe about themselves and other people. Everyone feels strongly about schools. Everyone has stories to tell, opinions to argue, theories to propound, anxieties to address.

As I've been describing, a young person's sense of self develops in relation to other people and also develops in relation to a surrounding environment. Wolf (1988) writes that we're born with certain innate potentials which are our biological heritage: 'However, it is the interaction with the environment that will evoke some of these potentials and bring them into development, whereas others are left to atrophy or may even be destroyed' (p.32). I want to explore the nature of the relationship between young people and the environment where – love it or hate it – they spend a large part of their lives.

But 'school' is a slippery idea. Young people lambasting 'school' are sometimes referring to an internalised school, a school stored in their unconscious minds where thirteen, fourteen, fifteen or sixteen years of hope and disappointment are collected. At other times they're referring to an external school, a collection of buildings out there, populated by other people who exist in their own right and who have competing needs. Sometimes they're referring to the relationship between these two kinds of 'school'.

Here's a 'school' story. It's 7.30 in the morning and Alex is being shouted at by his mother.

'Get out of bed or you'll be late for school!' She does this more in hope than in expectation that Alex will rouse himself without her needing to shout again or go upstairs. 'Sometimes I feel like giving up,' she says to her friend in the kitchen. 'If his father was around and actually cared, he'd make sure he was getting to school on time. But what can you do? To be honest, *this school* doesn't seem that bothered about them being late.' Alex's mother is doing her best but has always hoped that her son's school will have a more persuasive effect on him than she feels she has at home.

A mile away, the school caretaker surveys classroom FL5. One of his cleaners – the woman who normally cleans FL5 – hasn't arrived this morning and Michael isn't surprised. Yesterday, in response to the state of the girls' toilets, she announced that, '*This school* needs to get its act together if it wants to keep its cleaners!' and today, he assumes, the cleaner is taking her revenge on *this school* for tolerating girls who behave in such unladylike ways. It's 7.45a.m. The students will be arriving in less than an hour. At a glance, room FL5 looks okay, so Michael moves on.

In another building, the headteacher, Derek, sits at his desk, composing a letter to a local businessman, once a student of the school, who's complained about the behaviour in the town centre of students from the school. 'In my day, *this school* was a place where you did as you were told,' the complaining letter reads, 'but perhaps I'm just old-fashioned?' Derek is irked by the sarcastic tone of the letter but has to compose a balanced reply because businessmen talk to each other and the school can't afford to lose their support.

His mind strays and he finds himself thinking about Gareth and Linda, his deputies. Gareth has become the tough guy in the school, the person who ends up sorting out the misbehaviour, while Linda seems to have been cast as the perpetual carer, defending students wherever possible and sometimes criticising the staff for an alleged lack of compassion. Derek can see both sides. He wants to create a school which combines the qualities of Gareth and Linda. At times, Gareth reminds him of his own father who would treat all family issues as if they were ultimately about rules, undermining Derek's long-suffering mother in her efforts to take everyone's feelings into account. His mother died the year before Derek started this, his first headship, and he's always imagined that she would share his vision of how a school should be. 'Under my leadership,' he told the governors who interviewed him, '*this school* will combine tolerance with discipline, kindness with determination.'

Alex is late, irritated that he's had little time to perfect his hair because of his sister's extended stay in the bathroom. He hurries along the pavement, irritated also with his mother's nagging and hoping that no one will notice his hair. 'I hate *this school*,' he mutters to his friend. 'No one's bothered – they're only interested in themselves!' Sometimes he wonders where his father lives and what he's like but Alex never mentions his father to anyone. 'All they're interested in is exams, exams, exams,' he goes on, 'exams and if you're late and if you're wearing their stupid uniform!' He never misses school but, at the same time, resents going because 'school' confronts him with a series of existential givens, like the fact that he's getting older and will have to negotiate some kind of deal with the future; like the fact that, in common with the rest of the species, he'll have to work to survive, and like the perplexing fact that he has free will and can make choices yet is reliant on other people.

It's 8.30a.m. and his form tutor, Jermaine, is trudging across to room FL5. Jermaine is tired, having stayed up until after midnight marking coursework. It's his fourth year at the school, his fourth year as a teacher and he wonders what the future holds. 'The trouble with *this school*,' he sometimes says to friends in the staffroom, 'is that there's no career progression. As long as you're doing the job and not complaining, no one's really bothered.' Jermaine's girlfriend is out of the country at the moment, travelling the world as part of her well-paid job and, unusually, he's heard nothing from her for the last two weeks.

Jermaine starts taking the register in room FL5, calling out the students' names.

Alex arrives and sits down. But something isn't right. He jumps up and his chair jumps with him, sticking to his trousers. 'Oh, my god!' There's stickiness all over the chair – probably as the result of someone spilling their drink the day before.

Everyone's laughing.

'Sit down, Alex!' Jermaine calls wearily. 'We're doing the register.'

But they're laughing.

'No way! There's shit all over this chair!'

'Alex, sit down! And don't swear!' Jermaine has no idea why Alex is jumping about. 'Sit down!'

But Alex is desperate to save face. 'No way!' He kicks his chair away and, when Jermaine threatens him with punishment, tells Jermaine to fuck off.

There's no going back. The story will have to continue. Incidents like this give young people vital information about themselves in relation to others and the world. How powerful am I? How powerful are other people? How much notice should I take of them? These questions preoccupy a small child playing with its mother and, later, playing with its friends. As children become teenagers, 'school' becomes a focus for the same questions.

Like Alex and his mother, like Michael, Derek and Jermaine, we all have what Stokes (1994) calls an institution 'in-the-mind', an internalised sense of 'school' which informs our opinions, reactions and behaviours, causing us to over-react sometimes or to get things out of proportion. That internalised sense of an institution is, as Hinshelwood (2001) argues, 'formed and deeply influenced by the early experience of [the] institution of parenthood' (p.82). Young people, teachers and parents inevitably bring their personal histories to bear whenever they speak vehemently about *this school* because 'school' so powerfully evokes for everyone an expectation of nurture, of being looked after by parent-figures whilst being in competition with sibling-figures. Alex's sense of 'school' is informed by a missing father and by a mother struggling to be firm. The 'school' his mother refers to is a father-figure who gets Alex to do as he's told. The cleaner's 'school' is a parent-figure taking other members of the family for granted. Derek's 'school' is based on an understanding of his mother's role in the family and Jermaine's 'school' is another parent-figure, unconcerned about Jermaine's professional progress.

Primitive feelings, conflicts and dilemmas are enacted every day on the school campus which, in many ways, have nothing to do with an external school 'out there' but to which that external school must react, as Jermaine, *in loco parentis*, must now react to Alex's swearing. *This school* becomes a way of talking about things which are far more important than school. For example, a young person fighting at home with his parents typically announces in counselling that '*This school's* really doing my head in!' while another, after months of talking with me about how her warring parents could ever have loved each other, concludes, '*This school's* better now than it used to be!' Another talks about his inconsistent parents, saying, 'It's not all the teachers I don't get on with. Just some of them!' Still another is wary of talking about her childhood. 'Starting school seems like such a long time ago,' she says. A young person's perennial complaint that 'There's no point in school!' might really be a way of trying to talk about the point of anything, the point of being alive, whilst 'No one's bothered – they're only interested in themselves!' might be Alex's unconscious attempt to talk about his parents.

In my experience, young people regularly use *this school* as a way of talking about mothering. Every day at home, they're learning to live with the necessary imperfection of their mothers and so, predictably, the school down the road turns out to be another disappointing kind of mother. 'No one cares about you at *this school*! *This school's* only bothered about what other people think! It used to be good at *this school* but all the best teachers have left!' The vehemence of these generalisations and the fact that they're obviously felt so personally suggest that they're about more than just a collection of buildings.

I think it's probably true that, at an unconscious level, we view every organisation – even the world itself – as a sort of 'mother' by whom we expect to be looked after or ignored. Schools so readily become mother-like in the minds of young people because any institution concerned with the care and development of young people is bound to be an unconscious reminder of that original carer. I'm not suggesting that 'school' is literally a mother but that young people's experience of external school is related to their internalised experience of mothering. By 'mothering' I mean an abiding sense of being recognised, understood, looked after, admired, loved. Young people's relationship with 'school' becomes an unconscious and, at times, unsatisfactory relationship with an original mother-figure who recognises or doesn't, who understands or doesn't. I know that 'school' sometimes feels father-like as well and, at different times, is an oblique way of talking about particular issues such as childhood, authority or power. The idea of 'school' can even be used as a way of talking about death because *this school* easily ends up being about getting older and wondering what's-the-point, about saying goodbye and wondering whether we'll be remembered. But, more often, our internalised 'school' – the one young people complain so much about, the one that's *so* unfair, the one that *never* listens – is bound up with an experience of mothering.

I'm arguing that 'school' exists in the eye of the beholder, yet there really *is* an external school out there as well – a set of buildings populated by individuals who exist in their own right and inevitably affect one another. The bricks and mortar, the concrete and glass buildings exist independently of people (once people have designed and built them) and the layout, the architecture, the external *look* of a school have a powerful effect on young people.

After the House of Commons (another object of intense public projection) was damaged by bombs in 1941, Winston Churchill advocated its immediate re-building, arguing that 'We shape our buildings, and afterwards our buildings shape us.' Young people create a school-in-their-minds, an internalised sense of 'school' but are also shaped by the external buildings out there called 'school'. There's increasingly well-researched evidence about the effect of architecture on people's sense of well-being and mental health (Halpern 1995; Weich *et al.* 2002). Buildings looking as if they've been built to last, their weather-beaten stone promising permanence and resilience, or buildings looking well cared for with soft furnishings and warm colours are bound to affect and shape the way people feel about themselves.

I went to a school with impressive, old buildings readily suggesting authority and permanence. But, as I got older, these same buildings came to represent immovability and resistance to change. The traditions, rituals and ceremonies of the school could seem reassuringly familiar or coldly alienating. This external school had an effect on me but that effect was always informed by my internalised sense of what *this school* meant. And the meaning of *this school* changed according to how I was feeling at any particular moment about myself and other people.

I went off to teach in a very different kind of school with pre-fabricated classrooms which, because they were cheap, could be decorated and changed to suit my students without anyone objecting but which, precisely *because* they were cheap and impermanent, probably sent an implicit message to many students about their importance in the eyes of the world.

There's always a relationship between our internalised sense of *this school* and the external school we see 'out there'. Winnicott

(1965) describes an 'object-mother' as distinct from an 'environment-mother'. An 'object-mother' is essentially an *internalised* experience of mothering whereas an 'environment-mother' is an *external* kind of mothering, a mother 'who wards off the unpredictable and who actively provides care in handling and in general management' (p.75). External school readily slips into the role of environment-mother, organising and supervising, trying to take care of all her children and keep them safe. The external school face looking down may be of weather-beaten stone or pre-fabricated plasterboard: young people will react, in part, according to what they've *always* seen in such a face – the ability or inability to understand their needs, an internalised experience of mothering, a school-in-their-minds – but they'll also react according to a developing sense of what a face made of weather-beaten stone or pre-fabricated plasterboard looks like now that they're no longer children. The relationship between internalised and external 'school' is constantly changing. Something that once looked permanent and authoritative might now look immoveable and resistant to change without actually altering its physical appearance at all.

Wherever we are, we look to see ourselves reflected, we look to recognise ourselves, we look to make sense of ourselves through our surroundings. In part, we see what we've always seen, the projections of our internal world, but we also see new possibilities, new understandings of old experiences. Kellerman (2007) writes:

> Every environment is sending a subliminal message to us, indicating that we are either part of it or separated from it. People...search in nature for the kinds of mirroring influences that they need at certain times in their lives – from the trees in the forest, the waves of the ocean, the open views at the mountain-top, the desolate silence of the desert or the bustle of urban locations. These are places where we...can enjoy the environmental mirroring. (p.87)

Mirroring begins at birth when a baby looks to its mother's face for confirmation of its existence and for a recognition of its needs. Her face is everything. Everything depends on how she reacts. If she fails to recognise her baby or fails to understand its needs, then the baby is in danger.

Young people respond unconsciously to teachers as if they were mothering-figures because teachers have the same capacity and are in a similar position to enrage or contain, provoke or soothe. Like mothers, teachers mirror young people back to themselves, constantly providing feedback – affirmation, approval, criticism, disapproval – and constantly receiving feedback themselves from young people. They can be wonderfully attuned mothering-figures, listening carefully, trying their hardest to understand while, at other times, they haven't a clue. And teachers differ, providing wildly varying kinds of feedback.

The baby or young person absorbs all of this and, through the mirroring process, develops a sense of self – what I look like, how I sound, what I can do, what gets me approval or disapproval – in short, who I am. Young people need this feedback almost as urgently as a baby needs the response from its mother. Usually, the feedback reassures and comforts but sometimes it confuses and scares. Either way, young people need it, need it badly and yet resent needing it because needing anything from anyone leaves them vulnerable, should that person not be able to recognise or meet their needs. In that sense, they always approach the school gates warily, always with mixed feelings, wanting to be recognised and looked after by the institutional mother but fearing that she may be busy, irritable or distracted. They look for her in the face of her buildings and in the faces of her teachers. They're no longer babies but they're still dependent on the way this environment responds, 'How do I look? Does this look okay?'

They see different kinds of mothering. According to young people, boring lessons always seem to happen in boring classrooms, for example. I don't know whether the physical environment makes the lesson seem boring or whether the quality of the lesson makes the environment seem boring: what matters is that there's a relationship between the two. Every teacher and every architect (Ulrich 1984) knows that the colours, the pictures, the light, the view from the windows, the way in which you arrange your classroom furniture will all have a bearing on students' behaviour. Teachers go to great lengths to improve these things. But sometimes the physical improvements make absolutely no difference because the which-comes-first relationship between a bored feeling and a boring environment is like the which-comes-first relationship between a baby and its mother. They exist in relationship to one another. Never as separate entities.

And this is where an internalised, subjective sense of *this school* and an external, objective school come together for young people, where even magnolia walls covered with fading displays of work about the French Revolution, a torn map of the world and a laminated copy of the school rules can end up feeling mother-like. Winnicott (1971) describes our daily struggle 'in the perpetual human task of keeping inner and outer reality separate yet interrelated' (p.2). Despite fourteen or fifteen years' experience, some young people will tend to see in their environment what they've always seen in a mother's face and will react accordingly. The obvious difference between a teacher's face and the face of a classroom is that the face of a classroom is unmoved by anything. For many young people, this doesn't matter because they've grown up seeing benevolent or benign mothering wherever they look, even in tatty magnolia walls. But for others – less confident, less sure – the lack of a response is unsettling. It's what makes a classroom seem 'boring' and makes some students want to attack and vandalise it, as if they were trying to get a response – any response – from it. The unresponsiveness of the classroom is readily attributed to whichever teacher happens to be presiding who's then accused of 'not being interested' or of being a 'boring' teacher. 'No one's bothered,' says Alex to his friend on the way to school. 'They're only interested in exams, exams, exams!'

Typically, the walls of room FL5 have remained unmoved but, above the laughter of the other students, Jermaine has heard Alex swear. 'What did you say, Alex?'

'You heard!'

'Well, I'm sorry but I won't be spoken to like that. That's not the kind of language we tolerate at *this school*.'

Alex shrugs. 'See if I care!'

'Well, you will!' warns Jermaine. 'Go to the reception office and wait there.'

Neither of them wants this. Jermaine actually likes Alex but Alex has provoked feelings inside Jermaine about a faraway girlfriend not behaving as he'd expected. For his part, Alex has no real quarrel with Jermaine. Alex's real quarrel is with his father but he was feeling irritable when he sat down and then everyone laughed.

He makes a public show of being angry, calling out to Jermaine as he leaves the classroom, 'You know what? You can stick *this school* right up your arse!' He goes off to the reception office, scared about what will happen next.

Buildings, classrooms and teachers mirror young people back to themselves but all the people in Derek's school serve as mirrors for each other because we tend to see ourselves reflected in the members of any group that we happen to be in (Foulkes 1964). Young people make friends or enemies according to whatever they see of themselves mirrored in their peer group, constantly defining and re-defining themselves in terms of who they're like and who they're not like.

As the members of a group interact, relationships change and people see new things in each other: they're drawn closer or pushed further apart. They also become aware of and start referring to something called 'the group' in the same way that young people start referring to *this school*. Kohut (1976) describes the gradual emergence of a 'group self' made up of complementary characters and characteristics analogous to an individual self – a self made up (as I've described in Chapter 3) of roles or 'selves'. Individuals can describe their relationship with this group-as-a-whole as well as with each member of it. Sometimes 'the group' feels very safe and supportive while, at other times, it feels tense and difficult. Sometimes it feels loving, sometimes persecutory. The relationship between our internal and external worlds is always changing. 'The group' is changed by the people in it who are changed by 'the group'.

This school is really a group anthropomorphised, given human characteristics. Young people speak of 'school' *as if* 'school' were a person. Stacey (2006) writes that 'People have a tendency to individualise and idealise a collective and treat it "as if" *it* had overriding motives and values' (p.199). With its many student and teacher members, the feelings provoked by a school 'group' of a thousand people are intense, whether they're feelings of loyalty and affection or loathing and mistrust. It's easy to find a person or a cluster of people who seem to represent aspects of ourselves that we like or dislike. So when young people admire or despise *this school*, it may well be because they see aspects of themselves in the mirror of the school group. Often they're encouraged by what they see there while, at other times, they share Dracula's opinion of mirrors.

Schools become self-like as well as mother-like because self and mother were once inseparable ('There's no such thing as a baby'). A sense of self begins to emerge out of a first mothering relationship and the buildings and the classrooms all around, the teachers in front and the peers alongside are all reminders for young people of an original, internalised, mirroring mothering-figure who retains her power to present affirming, attractive reflections of those young people or critical, ugly ones. This power makes young people anxious. They badly need her approval but can't take it for granted. 'I don't care, anyway!' they say. '*This school* used to be okay but it's rubbish now!'

There are two ways in which young people resist this power, protecting themselves from the mirror's gaze. One way is to idealise *this school* with its buildings, teachers and peers, seeing in it the wonderfully kind and loving mothering-figure that some of them have never experienced but have always longed for. They wear their uniform with pride. They volunteer for everything. They appear to have no doubts about 'school' and no mixed feelings. In effect, they're telling 'school' that she's the best mother. Trying to be her perfect child is a way of keeping such a powerful mother sweet and a way of bolstering their own sense of being loveable.

But Klein (1956) warns that 'idealisation is a corollary to persecutory anxiety – a defence against it' (p.217). The powerful, longed-for mother may withdraw her favours at any moment. So an alternative and sometimes safer way of resisting her power is to demonise *this school*. A young person with an unhappy internalised sense of 'school' or simply full to the brim with longing for recognition and understanding might find it impossible to trust an external school promising these things – a school where the teachers are kind and consistent, where the older students are relaxed and friendly, where the opportunities are many and everyone knows your name. If *this school* is mother-like, then hating *this school* is sometimes a safer bet than trusting it.

So when young people talk about hating-school or rubbish-school or I-can't-wait-to-leave-school or you-can-stick-this-school-right-up-your-arse, they don't necessarily mean the school they attend every day. It's not as personal as it feels. It's just an insurance policy, a defence, a way of dealing with a mother-figure's power and not to be taken at face value. Eventually things do change: young people get and give feedback which changes them and changes the institution around them. Then, once they begin to realise – slowly, very slowly – that the greetings are unfailingly friendly and the warmth is genuine – hey presto! – the buildings no longer seem to frown and disapprove, *this school* seems to be smiling back and they find themselves admitting (even on the day they leave) that '*This school's* okay, really!'

Farida, the receptionist, puts down the phone. Already this morning she's fielded calls from a parent, angry about the bullying of her child the day before; from a salesman, wanting to visit the school to promote a new kind of software; from a member of the public reporting an incident half an hour ago on a school bus; from another parent, wanting to take his daughter skiing the following week, and from one of the governors, asking for the minutes of a meeting.

Farida loves her job. For the first time in her life, she feels as if she belongs and is appreciated. '*This school's* the best place I've ever worked in,' she tells everyone. She doesn't tell them about her violent ex-husband or about the constant insecurity of her childhood, travelling around army bases. 'People at *this school* really know how to look after each other,' she tells them.

A student comes into the reception office. 'I've been told to come here,' he says glumly.

She asks who sent him.

'My tutor.'

'Why did he send you?'

'I don't know. He just told me to come here.'

'Because you've done something wrong?'

'Probably!'

She tells Alex to sit down while she phones Jermaine.

Like all teachers, Jermaine is in a difficult position. He knows that Alex's outburst was probably fuelled by things which have got nothing to do with room FL5 or Jermaine himself but he also knows that rules are rules and, without them, nothing works. Alex broke a rule.

Farida manages to get hold of Jermaine, hears the story and promises to contact Gareth, the deputy headteacher, to say that Alex has been sent to the reception office for swearing at his tutor.

Gareth is about to go and teach a class when he gets Farida's phone call. He's irritated that Jermaine, whom he regards as a soft touch, couldn't defuse or deal with the situation himself because now Gareth has to act. It was he who insisted that all incidents of swearing at teachers should automatically result in students being excluded. 'We have to get the basics right at *this school*,' he argued at a senior management meeting. 'There has to be a level of respect.' Gareth is proud to be a deputy headteacher, having left school himself with few qualifications and having worked hard in his early adult life to catch up. 'There's no substitute for hard work and discipline,' he said at the meeting, 'but I worry that there are people in *this school* who don't necessarily share that belief.' At the time, he didn't look across the table at his fellow deputy, Linda, but he had her in mind. Linda, he knew, had been to a top university and sailed through life but it was Linda who never seemed to be around when students were being rude to staff or refusing to do as they were told.

He sets his class some work, apologises for leaving them yet again and goes across to the reception office where he's been told that Alex is waiting.

In the meantime, Linda was passing and heard about the incident from Farida. She knows Alex and is concerned that excluding him will only make things worse for a student capable of getting good grades, whose father is long gone and whose mother is struggling with depression. Although Linda was academically successful herself, she grew up experiencing none of the warmth she offers to her students. Linda's parents pushed her to succeed but she was left feeling somehow empty. 'I want *this school* to be a place where the students feel safe and feel that they're valued,' she responded at the meeting when Gareth made his pitch about hard work and discipline. 'If they're not going to be loved at home, then where will they be? And without that, they've got nothing!'

She and Gareth glared at each other across the table.

Linda suspects that Gareth will over-react and has intercepted Alex. She's taken him into another room where he's telling her that things between him and his mother are not good at the moment.

Gareth arrives at the reception office and asks Farida where Alex has gone. When she tells him, he erupts. 'The trouble with *this school*,' he mutters, 'is that students are indulged when what they need are clear boundaries!'

Farida has learned to say nothing.

'Whatever they say about our exclusion statistics,' he goes on, '*this school* cannot afford to tolerate rudeness to staff. Students have to learn to behave!'

Linda and Alex emerge together, smiling. 'Alex is going to apologise to his tutor,' Linda says to Gareth. 'It sounds as if it was just a bad start to the morning.'

The story will go on. Before the end of the morning, Gareth and Linda will both be in Derek's office, passionately arguing their points of view with Derek trying his best to bring them together, like the son he was, waiting patiently for the other members of the family to stop arguing.

He needs them both. In my experience, institutions not only become mother-like in the unconscious minds of young people but, like people, they develop the characteristics of a superego, id and ego (Freud 1923). In Derek's school, it's as if Gareth has come to represent the voice of the institutional superego –

forever critical, urging everyone on, never satisfied – while Linda has come to represent something of the institutional id – a swirl of inchoate, teenage emotion, likely to run amok at any moment. Gareth and Linda take on these roles because of their personal predispositions, their internalised schools, not because they're intellectually incapable of appreciating each other's position. Stokes (1994) writes, 'This is one unconscious reason why we form and join organisations... Internal personal conflicts can be projected onto the interpersonal or even inter-institutional stage' (p.124).

All schools contain the same polarities, as if the institutional psyche needs them. I've never worked in a school, for example, where certain staff haven't worried that the behaviour of students is getting worse. And with this come attendant worries – that staff morale isn't what it used to be, that the headteacher has no idea what's going on, that students are more promiscuous than they used to be, parents less supportive and colleagues less professional. In short, the institutional id seems to be out of control. Nor have I worked in a school where another group of staff in another corner of the staffroom haven't worried that there's an opposite drift towards discipline for discipline's sake. Students are no longer being listened to, they say. Too many are being excluded unnecessarily and 'We're becoming a police force rather than a school!' In short, the institutional superego appears to be riding roughshod over everyone.

I'm not suggesting that there's never any objective truth in these worries. Sometimes they're well-founded, though making that assessment will depend partly on the internalised 'school' of the person making it. My point is that intra-psychic, interpersonal and inter-institutional conflicts are 'dramatised' (Hinshelwood 2001) every day in schools. At one level, Alex's behaviour dramatises an argument in his own head between I'm-cared-for and I'm-not-cared-for: an attempt to make sense of his father. His behaviour also dramatises spectacularly the argument between Gareth and Linda – both personally *and* in terms of what they've come to represent for the institution. Obholzer and Roberts (1994) write that: 'This unconscious suction of individuals into performing a function on behalf of others as well as themselves happens in all institutions' (p.131). Teachers are habitually characterised by students as 'too strict' or 'not strict enough' and these internalised, parental polarities are enacted every day in classrooms, playgrounds and corridors. Everyone looks for some kind of balance to be struck by *this school* which so often becomes synonymous with 'headteacher'. Derek's job is to be the Freudian ego, holding everything in balance, including Gareth and Linda, allowing his deputies to keep thinking without getting stuck in their polarised roles and without enacting whatever they've come to represent for the institution. He also has to make sure that Alex isn't treated only in terms of what he represents – for Gareth, a dangerously unresolved breach of the rules and, for Linda, an example of unforgivable emotional neglect.

He hatches a plan.

'I think you do an extremely difficult job,' he says, sitting alone with Gareth over coffee, reviewing Gareth's innumerable responsibilities, 'because you're the person who ends up doing so much of the dirty work in *this school*.'

'You can say that again!'

'And I don't know why that's happened.'

Gareth volunteers a brief account of his years at the school and Linda's apparent reluctance to involve herself in disciplinary matters.

Derek's heard all this before and doesn't react. 'How would you like your role to expand, Gareth?'

'Expand! You're joking! I'm already fully stretched.'

'I know you are. And you're excellent at what you do. But I'd like the school to benefit from the other sides of you as well – your softer sides, if you like.'

'What d'you mean, "my softer sides"?'

'Your kindness, your sense of humour, your ability to empathise with students – all the sides of you that people don't see so often because of the role you've ended up playing.'

'I think people see those sides of me every day!' says Gareth. 'At least, I hope they do!'

'I'm sure they do,' Derek says, 'but you'd probably agree that there's an unfair perception of you as the person who does all the discipline.'

'You're right. There is. But someone's got to do it!'

'I know. And why should it always be you?'

'Why indeed!'

'I think the rest of us should be doing more of that stuff,' Derek says, 'letting you work more closely with the students so that they don't have this unfortunate perception of you as the Big Baddie!'

Gareth laughs. 'If only they knew! I used to be shy.'

'Really?'

'When I was at school nobody knew I was there!' He tells Derek a little about his childhood and his parents' lack of interest in their son's education. 'That's why I became a teacher – to make damn sure that the quiet ones like me were achieving what they were capable of achieving.'

Derek listens and suggests that, from now on, Gareth handles only the behaviour of the older students with Linda concentrating on the younger ones. 'That way, Gareth, you won't be endlessly besieged and you'll have more time to concentrate on the things you enjoy.'

Gareth looks relieved, relaxing into his chair.

Later, Derek meets with Linda.

'The students are very fond of you, Linda.'

She beams back. 'And I'm very fond of them.'

'I know. And I'm aware of how much of your time is devoted to supporting them.'

'Well, someone's got to do it!'

'You're right,' Derek says. 'And I'd like to free you up a little because I think that you and Gareth are both working your socks off.' He tells her the plan whereby she'll concentrate on younger students. 'This way, you'll have fewer students needing you and you'll be able to devote yourself to them without being so stretched. And, this way, you'll be responsible for everything – their behaviour, their support, their discipline – the lot.'

Linda meets his eye. 'Our exclusion statistics might go down!'

'Fine,' Derek says, refusing to be drawn into a discussion with her about Gareth, 'just as long as the students are behaving.'

She looks worried. 'I hate excluding them, Derek.'

'I know you do. And so do I. But I guess that's part of loving them, isn't it?'

She's never heard him talk about love before. She's heard Derek talk about kindness, consideration, tolerance, compassion, care, support. She's heard him talk about these things in assemblies, in staff meetings, in meetings with parents – endless meetings. But never about love. She smiles and says that she's looking forward to the change.

Derek hopes this will make a difference but knows perfectly well that, in a school, the potential split between 'discipline' and 'care' will never go away. As headteacher, he'll always be the one containing the split, the dissatisfactions, the unrealistic expectations, the constant need for his approval.

And the strong feelings. Because a school's preoccupation with whether or not to exclude students like Alex is also a preoccupation with strong feelings – rage, hatred, envy, despair – and whether they can ever be borne by *this school*. Menzies Lyth (1988) writes that people in trouble:

> are likely to provoke powerful and primitive feelings and
> fantasies in staff who suffer painful though not always
> acknowledged identifications with clients, intense reactions
> both positive and negative to them, pity for their plight, fear,
> possibly exaggerated, about their violence, or harsh, primi-
> tive, moral reactions to their delinquency. (p.230)

Teachers can't help becoming mothering-figures and, like
mothers, they absorb and feel their children's feelings. Like
mothers, they hate feeling that their best efforts aren't good
enough. They hate it when students point out their inadequa-
cies. And this happens a lot, provoking a simmering rage in some
teachers which sometimes ends in a student being excluded over
some incident because *unconsciously* the teacher's own rage, helplessness and frustration have become too much to bear. For
teachers, excluding a student can be like self-harming – a
blood-letting, a temporary relief from the unbearably strong
feelings provoked by a student's behaviour. Alex's behaviour
provokes feelings which Jermaine would rather not feel because
Jermaine would also like to tell a few people to fuck off. In
Jermaine's unconscious fantasy, excluding Alex will make these
feelings go away. The incident provokes feelings in Gareth
which Gareth would rather not feel – feelings from the past
about things getting out of control and about what it's like when
adults don't take enough responsibility for this. In Gareth's
fantasy, excluding Alex will make these feelings go away. And
the incident provokes feelings in Linda which Linda would
rather not feel – feelings of helplessness and what it's like to be
unloved. For her, excluding Alex will only make these feelings
worse.

Because of her intervention, Alex hasn't been excluded but
Derek is well aware that Linda's intervention has set an
uncomfortable precedent. So, in case other students should be
inclined to copy Alex, he needs everyone to realise the
seriousness of the incident.

He meets with Alex's mother himself. 'I think everyone at *this school* wants the best for Alex,' he says to her, 'but we simply can't tolerate rudeness to staff.'

She feels intimidated in Derek's office, reminded of her own unhappy schooldays. 'I don't know what it is about *this school*,' she insists, 'because we've had no problems with him at home.'

Derek's heard this many times before and knows that it's rarely true. He wants to support Alex's mother but, at the same time, needs her to appreciate that Alex has been very lucky not to be excluded.

'We'll continue to do all that we can to support him,' he says, 'but I'm sure you'll want to make it absolutely clear to Alex that swearing at a member of staff is against the rules. And I'm afraid that if it happens again, he'll be out.'

She nods. 'I don't know what it is with kids these days,' she says. 'He was always polite when he was little.'

'Well, I'm sure we've all made mistakes when we were younger,' Derek says. 'Just as long as he doesn't make the same mistake again.'

He shows Alex's mother out of the room and returns to his pile of work, hoping that Linda's intervention won't cause further problems in the weeks to come. For the record, he writes a brief letter to Alex's mother, recording their conversation and making the school's position absolutely clear.

He puts his energies into these things every day – calming people down, sorting out their mistakes, endlessly watching over the balance between 'discipline' and 'care' as it tilts one way and then the other – well aware that some of the governors think he should be doing more to improve the school's public image because there are always local businessmen and politicians to pacify, journalists to enthuse, prospective parents and teachers to attract to the school and, under pressure from these people, schools often end up re-branding themselves with a new, corporate colour, new logo, new website and new prospectus.

These changes will give everyone a clearer sense of purpose, it is announced. And from now on, the students will all wear a new, smarter uniform to encourage in them a sense of belonging.

Derek does his best to resist these pressures. He knows perfectly well that initiatives like these have their place but that 'belonging' to a school is a far subtler experience. Young people feel that they belong when they can accept that the internalised school in their minds and the external school they attend will always be a bit of a mixture; when they can accept that the institutional mother will never be perfect and that their feelings about her will always be mixed. They scratch their names onto her desks as vandalism (I want to destroy *this school*) and as affection (I want to remain part of *this school*). When they can tolerate such mixed feelings without having to enact them in these ways, then they can relax and enjoy a sense of belonging because what they're really belonging to is themselves, to *all* of themselves, the good feelings as well as the bad. It's as if all their time in front of the mirrors of *this school* is in order to achieve this simple, desperate end: 'At last I see the world as it is and me reflected back as I am – as a bit of a mixture. At last I belong. At last I'm me.'

The stories we tell about ourselves also serve as mirrors. 'At Last I'm Me' could almost be the title of a young person's autobiography. We tell stories about our lives, as I've described in Chapter 2, and the extent to which we tell our auto-biographical stories in chronological, coherent, thoughtful ways is an indicator of the extent to which we can function as coherent, thoughtful selves. Families also tell autobiographical stories ('We're a wonderfully close-knit, loving family!') which are never entirely reliable, as everyone knows, so alternative versions are told in hushed tones and behind closed doors. The importance of family stories is that they function as mirrors into which family members look to recognise themselves: 'Is this the family to which I belong? Do I recognise myself in this family story?'

All schools tell stories about themselves. The oldest schools even have their stories written down and bound into books as Official Histories ('The Story of *This School*'). The official school story is told formally on public occasions in prizegivings, assemblies, press releases and newsletters while alternative versions are told in private.

Young people look into the mirror of the school story to recognise themselves but the problem is that most schools tell at least two very different stories. The first is The Bullshit Story and it never varies. In a condensed version, it goes:

> This is an excellent school, improving year after year. This year's results were even better than last year's and next year's results will be even better than this year's. This happens because we all care passionately, all work very hard indeed and are all very talented.

This story emerges because new headteachers are often keen to put their stamp on a school. From now on, *this* is the story we'll be telling ourselves, they insist. The past is dead. History has been re-written. We have a new story to tell. To some extent, schools are obliged to tell The Bullshit Story in response to political pressures. But everyone knows it's a bullshit story – an unreliable mirror – because it doesn't make sense of everyone's daily experience where things *don't* always go smoothly, where progress *isn't* incremental and where things are *not* always for the best in this best of all possible schools.

I'm not suggesting that aspiration and excellence aren't important, nor am I suggesting that complacency and under-achievement are ever acceptable. But not everyone is capable of everything and 'bullshitting' or telling young people that they can achieve anything if only they try hard enough is unfair (see Chapter 5). They can't.

The problem with The Bullshit Story is that it creates anxiety. Living with its grandiosity is unsettling because, when the story is finally exposed and breaks down, as everyone knew it would, the breakdown can feel like a terrible failure. Despite everyone's hard work, the predictions haven't come true, the unrealistic targets haven't been met and the latest report about the school is critical. Potentially, a school is left with the flip side of its grandiosity – despair. But the headteacher responsible for propagating The Bullshit Story has left by now and someone else is trying to pick up the pieces, beginning to construct a more realistic story which takes account of the school's frailties as well as its strengths.

There's a second story. The Story of The Golden Age looks backwards rather than forwards. It remembers the big flood, thirty years ago, when the pipes burst and everyone rallied round. It remembers the teacher who left in disgrace and the two who fell in love, got married and have only just retired from the staff. It remembers the fundraising which helped to build the current changing rooms, the wonderful teacher who died of cancer and the talented student who committed suicide. It remembers the summer fairs, the musicals, the eccentric librarian who kept falling asleep, the notorious ex-student who robbed a bank and the headteacher no one liked.

The Story of The Golden Age is told by parents (many of whom went to the school themselves) as well as by teachers, old and retired. It's a nostalgic, amusing, comforting story and, whereas The Bullshit Story seems to focus coldly on tasks, The Story of The Golden Age is proud to focus on the warmth of human relationships because 'they're what really matter'.

Neither of these stories is of much use to young people. The Bullshit Story makes them anxious and The Story of The Golden Age makes them feel as if they've missed out on something special. Again. But for the storytellers, they're attractive stories because they're so simple, attempting to bind everyone together, avoiding difference and promoting sameness. In the future, everyone *will* be successful. In the past, everyone *was* happy.

Our sense of well-being depends on the kind of story we're telling about ourselves – coherent or fragmented, realistic or grandiose, confident or merely nostalgic. The importance of a school story is that it functions as another kind of mirror into which young people look to recognise themselves. So when they look and see something unrecognisable, they're bound to feel nervous.

There's a third story to be told. This is a more useful story, focusing on tasks *and* relationships or what Fielding (2006) calls the 'functional' and the 'personal'. This story looks at the challenges ahead, at what must be done, but it also looks back fondly on the way things were and the contributions of so many people to the school. It accepts the importance of tasks but describes relationships as the way to get tasks done.

This third story is more varied, more flexible and, therefore, of more use to young people because it tells of failure as well as success, of things tried, mistakes made and lessons learned. It doesn't condone but it allows for mistakes and for people's shortcomings. This story makes sense to young people because, as they're always keen to point out, 'Shit happens!' This story celebrates difference. It allows for unpredictability and ambivalence. It acknowledges that schools, like people, have the potential to be destructive as well as creative (see Chapter 5). In this story, young people can recognise themselves because they can recognise something that's a bit of a mixture.

This is the story that Derek is trying to tell, resisting The Bullshit Story and resisting The Story of The Golden Age; resisting the temptation to prioritise between tasks and relationships, between 'functional' Gareth and 'personal' Linda. He tries to match the practical needs of the external school with the needs and complexity of a thousand internalised schools projected onto it. So, on the day of the 'Alex' incident, he makes a point of bumping into Jermaine.

'We haven't excluded Alex this time,' Derek explains, 'but he needs to know that what he did was wrong and that he shouldn't have sworn at you, whatever the reason.'

Jermaine agrees. Derek tells him to have a word with Alex as soon as possible and asks Jermaine how he's feeling.

'Okay,' Jermaine replies, 'plodding on...'

'Plodding?'

'Well, you know. Sometimes it gets a bit much.'

'Working so hard?'

'No, I don't mind hard work!'

'But you probably do mind being sworn at by students,' says Derek, 'especially when you're working flat out to help them!'

Jermaine agrees. 'You could say that!'

'So, how's life generally?'

'Average.'

'Only average?'

Jermaine doesn't want to say anything about his girlfriend, travelling the world, but does mention that he's been feeling stuck.

Derek asks what would help and, a week later, they meet in his office to agree some changes which will make Jermaine's work feel less 'plodding' in the future. These changes will suit the needs of the external school but will also address Jermaine's internalised school in which he needs to feel that he's making professional progress, keeping up with his girlfriend.

Feeling lighter after the first of these conversations, Jermaine catches up with Alex later that day. 'You were out of order this morning, Alex.'

Alex pulls a face. 'That chair was disgusting, sir!'

'That's right. It was,' says Jermaine, 'and you shouldn't have sworn.'

Alex says nothing.

'Should you?'

'No, sir.'

'How's life generally?' asks Jermaine, echoing Derek.

'Crap!'

'Go on…?'

Alex shrugs. 'What d'you want to know?'

'How's school?'

'Crap.'

'Home?'

'Crap.'

'Even with your mum?'

'Especially with my mum! She goes on at me all the time,' says Alex. 'Nagging all the time. Do this! Do that! Never stops.'

'And you feel like swearing at her?'

'Yeah!'

They both laugh, realising.

CHAPTER 5

A Potential Self

This book has been about a 'self' developing in relation to other people and an environment. It's been about the ways in which a 'self' gets damaged and repaired by relationships with those people and with that environment.

A young person gradually establishing a sense of 'who I am' is all very well, however. Parents, grandparents, teachers and other professionals are immediately interested in 'who you could be'.

They sit in a dingy classroom. Other young people are getting on with their work nearby. She likes him, realising that his reluctance to get on with his work is because of his lack of confidence. She knows a bit about his life at home and is determined to do her best to help him get as much as possible from school. That's why she's a teacher.

'This is stupid!'

She smiles. 'Why is it stupid?'

'Because it is! Because I can't do it!'

'You can if you try.'

'I can't. I'm telling you! I don't understand.'

'Give it a try.'

'I have tried! I can't do it. How many more times do I have to tell you?'

She knows not to respond immediately but lets him cool, waits, and, unflustered, explains again.

'I still don't get it!'

She hears the note of triumph in his voice but stays calm. 'What exactly don't you get?'

'Everything!' She looks disbelieving. He stares back at her. 'What?'

'I think you're being deliberately slow about this. It's not that difficult.'

'It is to me!'

'No, it's not. Look...'

'Don't bother,' he says. 'I'm not doing it!'

'Why not?'

'Because I'm not!'

'Because you're not?' She buys herself more time, repeating slowly, 'Because you're not...?' then, sidestepping, tries a new tactic. 'Look,' she says, 'you can refuse to do any work – that can be your choice – but I think that would be a real shame because you've got so much potential.'

She notices him flinch.

The idea of 'potential' is enshrined in the rhetoric of every classroom: potential is good, potential is exciting. Schools aim 'to develop the potential of every student'. Politicians aim to unlock the potential of whoever they aspire to lead. And countless young people are regularly invited to realise their 'full potential' by passionate, idealistic (if sometimes frustrated) adults, 'You've got so much potential!'

I want to explore why this exhortation falls on so many deaf ears and why it's actually debilitating for some young people.

She'd thought he'd be pleased to hear his potential recognised but, seeing him flinch, she asks, 'What's up?'

'Nothing.'

She wonders if he's remembered something upsetting. 'Are you okay?'

'Yeah.'

So she goes on, 'You've got the potential to make something of your life. You could do all kinds of things. You could do so much!'

He looks unconvinced.

'With a little effort and some decent exam results, you could go on to the sixth form or college or get a really good job.'

'Yeah,' he mutters, 'as if!'

She hears the sarcasm in his voice. 'You could!' she says. 'Really, you could!'

One of the problems with having 'so much potential' is that young people have the potential to be destructive as well as creative. They can be both. And, somewhere inside, they know it.

He shakes his head. 'No way could I do that!'

'You could, honestly!' Quickly she begins to enumerate his many abilities and qualities.

He looks embarrassed. 'You may think that stuff about me but you don't know me.'

By the time they become teenagers, most young people have bullied, hated, envied, lied. They've been violent and taken revenge. And these things have usually been pointed out to them in no uncertain terms. They're no longer perfectly formed, innocent sons and daughters, gurgling sweetly, but have joined the human race as necessarily flawed, complex citizens, motivated by noble and ignoble ends. The danger is that we persist with the idea that they can somehow all make a fresh start, that at sixteen the slate is wiped clean and they can start again with the world as their oyster.

I'm not suggesting that we should ever give up on young people or that they should be put into some box marked Failure and left to rot. I'm suggesting, rather, that an insistence on everyone's unlimited potential creates its own kind of box and the danger is that, instead of energising young people, it has the opposite effect.

> *'I think you have amazing potential.'*
> *He looks scornful. 'How d'you know?'*
> *'I can see it.'*
> *'Yeah?'*

Most young people are self-conscious, afraid of getting it wrong or being uncool. They agonise about how they're coming across to other people. When someone claims to 'see' their potential, they're confounded because they've put so much work into *not* being seen. They've been busily building up their defences over the years, so a person who claims to see through these defences is either frighteningly powerful or bluffing.

> *'How come you can see my potential?'*
> *'Because I know you.'*
> *'You must be a mind-reader then!'*
> *'I'm not. I just know what you're capable of.'*

Young people know that they have the potential *not* to fulfil their potential. They have the potential to waste time, to be ordinary, to fail. The more we eulogise their potential, the more anxious they become because they know that they have many kinds of potential – the potential to be cruel as well as kind, to be destructive as well as constructive.

Because the idea of their own potential is so contradictory, some young people become paralysed. They get called 'lazy' when really they're stuck, unable to move forward or back, unsure what to do. They complain that they're bored. Phillips (1993) describes that bored feeling as marking some kind of transition, a pause before moving on again. It may be that when young people are stuck and complain of being bored, they mean that they can find no focus, that they sense they should be doing something, that time is passing, but they have no idea what to do or how to be. In that sense, they're full of potential but the fullness is actually paralysing and, in any case, the wondrous abilities claimed for them often say more about the claimant than about anyone else.

She goes on: 'I can see it in the way you are with people. You're friendly, you're loyal, you want the best for people. You're artistic and good at practical things. You're talented in all kinds of ways!'

It's very hard to work or live with young people and not project one's own sense of unfulfilled potential onto them. I've often wanted to stop professionals and parents when they are in full spate, praising a young person's potential, and ask, 'To what extent do you think you've fulfilled your own potential?' because I suspect that, in many cases, the honest answer would be 'Not much'. When a professional's own sense of unrealised potential drives their work with young people, that work may be very productive, but the danger is that those young people most obviously *not* fulfilling their potential (or the potential adults see) can seem as if they're personally thwarting the professional. Instead, we could usefully ask ourselves, 'To what extent do I have the potential to help young people achieve theirs? How do I know that I have this potential? How will I come to terms with my inevitable limitations? Or will I blame the young people I'm working with for my own sense of limitation?'

'You've got your whole life ahead of you,' she says. 'Think about it! Think of the opportunities!'

It's equally hard to work with young people and not envy them their youth. They have so many opportunities nowadays, we observe ruefully, more opportunities than they know what to do with. There's a danger that our envy provokes us actually to punish young people by praising their limitless potential. Then we can attack them for wasting it.

   'It would be such a shame if you did nothing with all the abilities you've got,' she says.
   He looks blank.

Just as professionals have mixed feelings about young people's potential, I think that young people, in turn, envy the potential of children, about whom they are both fiercely protective and fiercely envious. It's as if young people can look back and see all the opportunities, all the potential that children still have. A child hasn't missed any opportunities. A child may turn out to have all sorts of talents. And children probably feel the same way about babies – passionately caring for them while resenting their very existence.

   'I haven't got any abilities,' he says.
   'Yes, you have!'
   He shakes his head, apparently amused.

Our belief in every young person's 'potential' may stem from the Romantic idealisation of the child trailing clouds of glory and containing endless, innate wonders, or it may stem from the belief that a person has a unique, core self which it is within that person's power to discover or 'actualise' (Maslow 1968). I think that for young people 'What I'm like now' and 'What I'm going to be like in the future' is more prosaic. It keeps changing and is expressed much more readily in terms of family. Ask any young person to talk about their family and they can describe ways in which they're like or unlike their mother or father, brother or sister. They can describe ways in which they plan to be like or unlike those people in the future, whereas an assertion such as 'You can choose who you want to be in your life!' sounds more like an invitation to a fancy dress party than any meaningful way of approaching a future which, to some extent, is already constrained by class, race, gender and all the effects of a family upbringing.

> *'What's to stop you doing something amazing with your life?'*
> *He snorts. 'Plenty!'*
> *'I think you can achieve your potential,' she says, 'provided you concentrate and don't let other people distract you.'*

I think there's an implied link between 'achieving your potential' and being unique, as if a person's potential has its own fingerprint. Television is preoccupied with talent shows designed to find the person out there with the X Factor, with 'what it takes'. And pundits claim to know what this is. Young people form queues around the block, waiting for the brief audition which will resolve the debate going on in their heads between I-am-ordinary and I-am-extraordinary. A lot hangs on this. The winners are wildly fêted while the losers slink away and a follow-up show highlights their most ridiculous failures – the singers who squawked, the dancers who fell over. These people are mocked for presuming to have potential. Aspiration is assumed to be very good but limitation is very bad. 'Reality' programmes and celebrity gossip magazines also explore the same debate about a person's ordinariness (bruises, spots, accidents, farts) or extraordinariness. Anyone cast for a while as extraordinary – a star – is eventually re-cast as an ordinary mortal as their marriage fails, they put on weight and enter re-hab. We get our disappointed revenge.

Most young people toy with the idea of being extraordinary or unique (having 'potential') before settling for the knowledge that they're probably much like other people. They admire and resent those still believing themselves to be unique because the idea of being unique, being different, being the best at something is frightening. It threatens to isolate young people when their most powerful ambition is to be loved and to belong.

> *'I'm not bothered about other people,' he says.*
> *She knows this isn't true – it never is – but says nothing.*
> *He goes on, 'It's up to me what I do with my life.'*

There's an assertion beloved of people with lots of money that 'You can achieve anything if you want it enough!' This makes life very simple, implying, first, that we can all do absolutely anything and, second, that wishing it will make it happen. The implication is that any limitations you may have are entirely your own fault. You didn't try hard enough. You didn't 'want it enough'. There's no allowance for not being good enough, for coming second or for the fact that dreams change in the light of experience. I think young people sense that it's not as simple as merely 'wanting it enough' and that they are already compromised by missed opportunities and by a lack of certain talents. I wonder whether they're always touched by the plight of disabled people – and they are – because they themselves feel implicitly disabled – no longer able to believe in the myth of their own omnipotence.

> *'Don't you want to do something with your life?'*
> *He shrugs. 'I'm happy the way I am.'*
> *'But surely you don't want to be like everyone else? What's so good about being the same?'*
> *'I like it,' he says, disarmingly. 'I don't want to be different.'*

When we implore young people to realise their individual potential, we put them in a difficult position. They are individuals but they exist also as members of groups and in relation to other people. They are part of as well as apart from, social as well as solitary. I remember a group of young people who went round together as a gang, all dressed the same way and calling themselves – wonderfully – The Individuals. Groups have their own collective potential to be supportive or persecutory, creative or destructive. It's hard for individuals to develop their creative potential unless there's a prevailing culture of creativity in the wider group. When young people protest that they can't do something, it's not necessarily because they're incapable but because the group culture can't allow it. Part of the challenge for professionals is how to realise the creative potential of young people *as a group*. There are peer support initiatives (Luxmoore 2000, 2002) which do this particularly effectively, drawing out the many positive qualities of young people and developing a creative group culture.

She looks at him and sighs. 'All I'm saying is that the future is out there and it's up to you to make the most of it.'

Talking with young people about the future is rarely straightforward. The future is exciting, for sure, especially if you feel confident about yourself and your abilities. But it's also frightening. And most young people *don't* feel confident about themselves or their abilities. They certainly don't feel as confident as they pretend. The future, we promise them, offers endless freedoms, exactly the kind of freedoms that they complain so vehemently about not having. But they already know enough about freedom to fear its implications. They know enough about free will and choice to know that choice brings independence but independence sometimes brings loneliness and always brings responsibility. Faced with the future, many young people regress. When the past has been chaotic, full of insecure attachments, broken promises and lies, they have to go back before they can go forward. They use the opportunity of counselling, for example, to recover and make sense of the past in order to move on. They remain ambivalent about the future. As each group of sixteen-year-olds prepares to leave school, their behaviour expresses their ambivalence as it swings between the very adult – working hard, planning ahead – and the very childlike – letting off fire alarms, flouting the rules. Under pressure themselves, professionals encourage young people to embrace the future 'before it's too late' but young people already know that time is limited. By the time they're sixteen, they've all been shocked by the death of someone they knew. They've been reminded of their own potential to die. So describing the future as a safe, linear progression (if you do that, this will happen and if you do this, that will happen) may convince some but for most it makes no sense because it avoids the really big questions: Will I matter? Will I be loved? Will there be any point in my life?

'That's what you think,' he says, 'and all I'm saying is that I don't want to do any of that.'

'What do you want to do?' she asks.

'I don't know!'

She realises that he's telling the truth. He really doesn't know. She tries to think what to say that will be helpful but feels at a loss. 'I feel bad,' she says, 'just leaving it like that.'

'Don't be. It's not your fault,' he says, sounding older than his sixteen years.

'But I feel as if I should be helping you more.'

'There's nothing you can do,' he says. 'It's not important anyway.'

'What is important?'

He looks uncomfortable. He can't answer but she knows already. If he could speak, he'd probably say that it's important to be liked – liked by his family, liked by his friends and even, possibly, loved by them. Then the immediate future would still be unclear but, in the long run, he'd be all right.

She knows this has to go unspoken. She can't embarrass him with words. Yet she wants to say so much. She wants to tell him about her own childhood, her own parents, the bad times, the loneliness and how things gradually got better. She wants to assure him that he matters. To her.

They look at each other.

'Can I go, Miss?'

She nods. 'Of course you can. But don't forget to get the work done.'

He smiles back. 'As if I would!'

References

Axline, V.M. (1966) *Dibs: In Search of Self.* London: Victor Gollancz.

Blos, P. (1962) *On Adolescence: A Psychoanalytic Interpretation.* New York: The Free Press.

Fielding, M. (2006) 'Naming the new totalitarianism: an examination of leadership, personalisation and high performance schooling.' *School Leadership and Management 26,* 4, 347–369.

Fonagy, P., Gergely, G., Jurist, E.J. and Target, M. (2004) *Affect Regulation, Mentalization, and the Development of the Self.* London: Karnac Books.

Foulkes, S.H. (1964) *Therapeutic Group Analysis.* London: George Allen & Unwin Ltd.

Freud, S. (1914) *On Narcissism.* Standard Edition, Volume 14. London: Hogarth Press.

Freud, S. (1923) *The Ego and the Id.* Standard Edition, Volume 19. London: Hogarth Press.

Gerhardt, S. (2004) *Why Love Matters: How Affection Shapes a Baby's Brain.* Hove: Brunner-Routledge.

Halpern, D. (1995) *Mental Health and the Built Environment: More Than Bricks and Mortar?* London: Taylor and Francis.

Hinshelwood, R.D. (2001) *Thinking About Institutions: Milieux and Madness.* London: Jessica Kingsley Publishers.

Holmes, J. (2001) *The Search for the Secure Base: Attachment Theory and Psychotherapy.* Hove: Brunner-Routledge.

Honneth, A. (1995) *The Struggle for Recognition: The Moral Grammar of Social Conflicts.* Cambridge: Polity Press.

Kellerman, P.F. (2007) 'Let's Face It: Mirroring in Psychodrama.' In C. Baim, J. Burmeister and M. Maciel (eds) *Psychodrama: Advances in Theory and Practice.* Hove: Routledge.

Klein, M. (1946) 'Notes on Some Schizoid Mechanisms.' In M. Klein, P. Heimann, S. Isaacs and J. Riviere (eds) *Developments in Psychoanalysis.* London: Hogarth Press.

Klein, M. (1956) 'A Study of Envy and Gratitude.' In J. Mitchell (ed.) *The Selected Melanie Klein.* London: Penguin Books.

Kohut, H. (1971) *The Analysis of the Self: A Systematic Approach to the Psychoanalytic Treatment of Narcissistic Personality Disorders.* New York: International Universities Press.

Kohut, H. (1976) 'Creativeness, Charisma, Group Psychology.' In J.E. Gedo and G.H. Pollock (eds) *Freud: The Fusion of Science and Humanism.* New York: International Universities Press.

Kohut, H. (1977) *The Restoration of the Self.* New York: International Universities Press.

Kohut, H. and Wolf, E.S. (1978) 'The disorders of the self and their treatment: an outline.' *International Journal of Psychoanalysis 59.* Re-printed in Morrison, A.P. (ed.) (1986) *Essential Papers on Narcissism.* New York: New York University Press.

Lomas, P. (1987) *The Limits of Interpretation.* London: Constable Publishers.

Luxmoore, N. (2000) *Listening to Young People in School, Youth Work and Counselling.* London: Jessica Kingsley Publishers.

Luxmoore, N. (2002) 'Can We Do Something? Young People Using Action Methods to Support Each Other in School.' In A. Bannister and A. Huntingdon (eds) *Communicating with Children and Adolescents.* London: Jessica Kingsley Publishers.

Maslow, A.H. (1968) *Towards a Psychology of Being.* New York: Van Nostrand.

Menzies Lyth, I. (1988) *Containing Anxiety in Institutions.* London: Free Association Books.

Mollon, P. (2002) *Shame and Jealousy: The Hidden Turmoils.* London: Karnac Books.

Mollon, P. (2005) *EMDR and the Energy Therapies.* London: Karnac Books.

Moreno, J.L. (1946) *Psychodrama, Volume 1.* Beacon, NY: Beacon House.

Obholzer, A. and Zagier Roberts, V. (1994) 'The Troublesome Individual and the Troubled Institution.' In A. Obholzer and V. Zagier Roberts (eds) *The Unconscious at Work.* London: Routledge.

Phillips, A. (1993) *On Kissing, Tickling and Being Bored.* London: Faber.

Plummer, D. (2007) *Self-esteem Games for Children.* London: Jessica Kingsley Publishers.

Rothschild, B. (2000) *The Body Remembers: The Psychophysiology of Trauma and Trauma Treatment.* New York: W.W. Norton.

Sayers, J. (1998) *Boy Crazy.* London: Routledge.

Stacey, R. (2006) 'Theories of Change in Therapeutic Work.' In *Clinical Child Psychology and Psychiatry. Vol 11.* London: Sage Publications.

Stern, D.N. (1985) *The Interpersonal World of the Infant.* New York: Basic Books.

Stokes, J. (1994) 'Institutional Chaos and Personal Stress.' In A. Obholzer and V. Zagier Roberts (eds) *The Unconscious at Work.* London: Routledge.

Storr, A. (1960) *The Integrity of the Personality.* London: Heinemann.

Ulrich, R.S. (1984) 'Aesthetic and Affective Response to Natural Environments.' In I. Altman and J.F. Wohlwill (eds) *Human Behaviour and Environment.* New York: Plenum Press.

Verhofstadt-Deneve, L. (2007) 'Existential-dialectic Psychodrama: The Theory Behind Practice.' In C. Baim, J. Burmeister and M. Maciel (eds) *Psychodrama: Advances in Theory and Practice.* Hove: Routledge.

Weich, S., Blanchard, M., Prince, M., Burton, E., Erens, B. and Sproston, K. (2002) 'Mental health and the built environment: cross-sectional survey of individual and contextual risk factors for depression.' *British Journal of Psychiatry 180*, 428–433.

Winnicott, D.W. (1964) *The Child, the Family and the Outside World.* London: Tavistock Publications.

Winnicott, D.W. (1965) *The Maturational Processes and the Facilitating Environment.* London: Hogarth Press.

Winnicott, D.W. (1971) *Playing and Reality.* London: Routledge.

Winnicott, D.W. (1975) *Collected Papers: Through Paediatrics to Psycho-analysis.* London: Tavistock Publications.

Wolf, E.S. (1988) *Treating the Self: Elements of Clinical Self Psychology.* New York: The Guilford Press.

Index